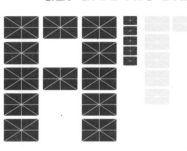

GB: GRAPHIC BRITAIN

LAURENCE KING

Published in 2002 by Laurence King Publishing Ltd
71 Great Russell Street
London WC1B 3BP
Tel: + 44 20 7430 8850
Fax: + 44 20 7430 8880
e-mail: enquiries@laurenceking.co.uk
www.laurenceking.co.uk

A catalogue record for this book is available from the British Library

ISBN 1 85669 311 2

Printed in Spain

Designed & illustrated by   email: bark@barkdesign.demon.co.uk

Assistant Editor: Stella Killery

The work featured in this book was selected by Patrick Burgoyne, *Creative
Review*; Marc Valli and Montse, Magma; and Vince Frost, Frost Design.

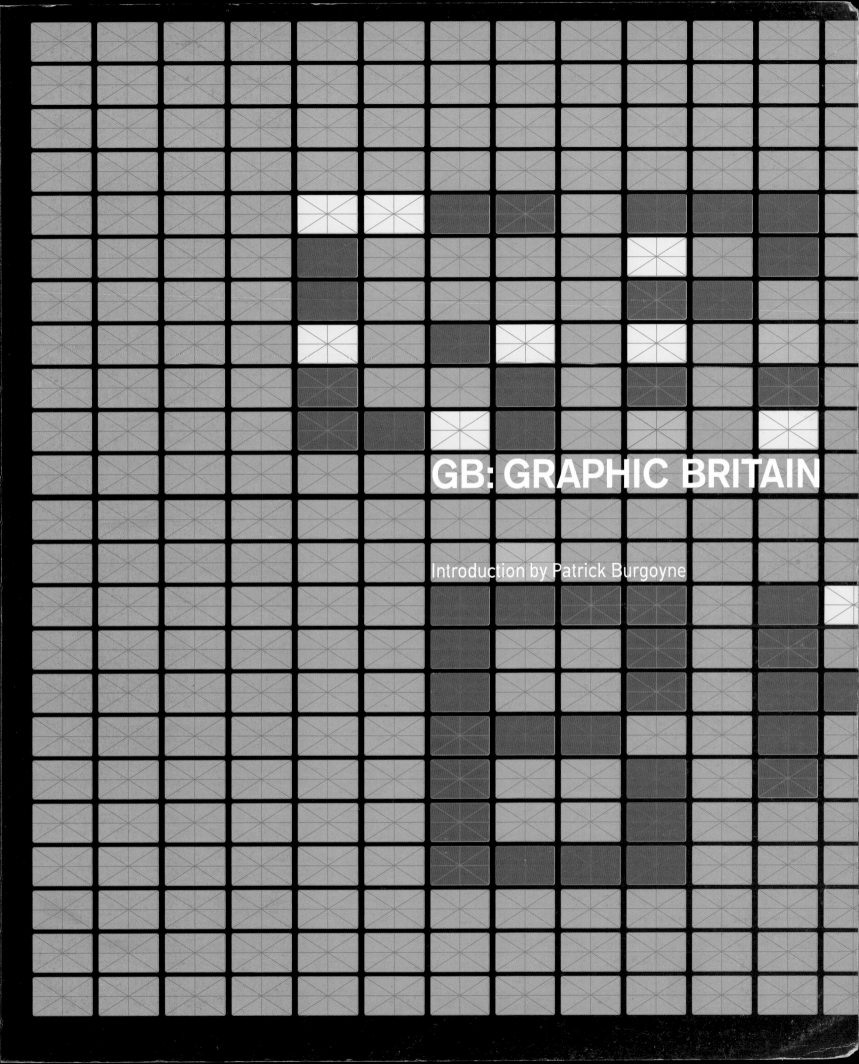

GB: GRAPHIC BRITAIN

Introduction by Patrick Burgoyne

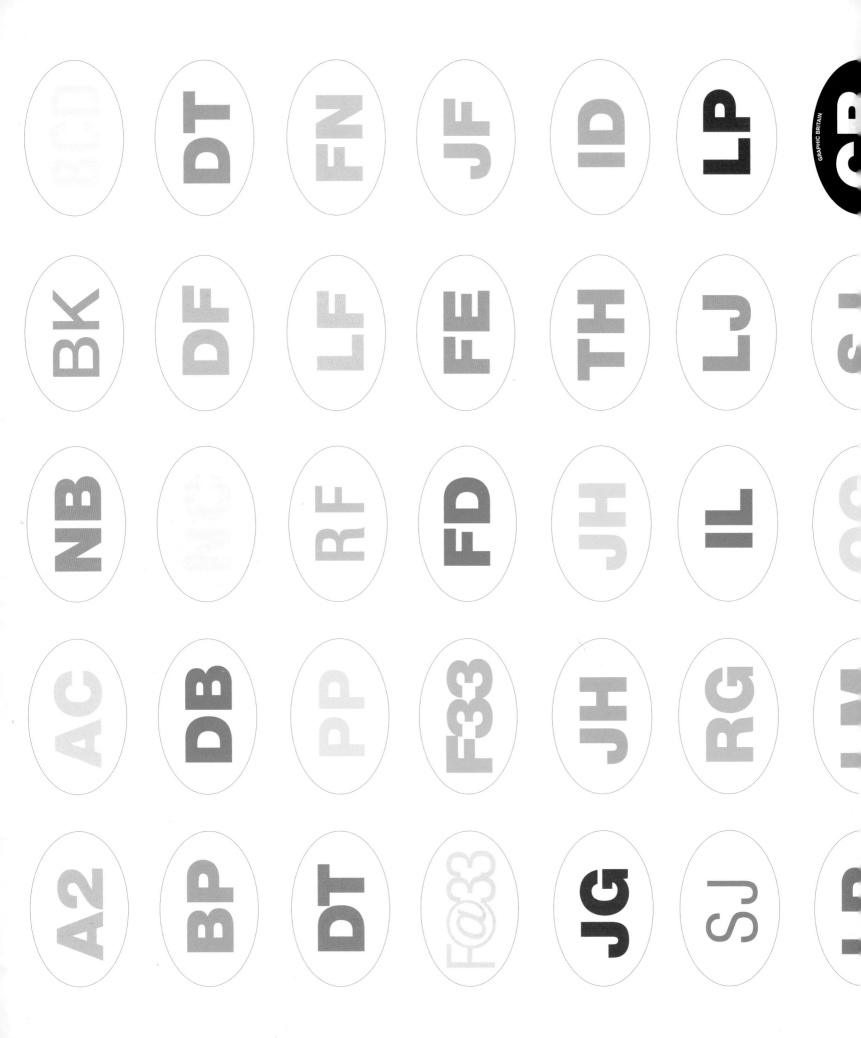

CONTENTS

INTRODUCTION

It is tempting to compartmentalize the history of graphic design into dominant movements and influential individuals: a neat timeline marks out Modernism, which begat the International Typographic Style, followed by Post-Modernism and Deconstruction. First Bauhaus, then Tschichold, followed by Müller-Brockmann and Rand, Brody and Carson. All nice and neat and, despite the oversimplification, valid as a basic, broad-brush overview.

By such logic, it would appear to be time for The Next Big Thing, time for someone or some group to step forward and introduce the next dominant graphic paradigm to an eagerly awaiting world. Britain has been home to many seminal figures in the history of graphic design, both in terms of its own citizens and those of other nations, who have found the country an inspiring and convivial place in which to work – from Schleger, Eckersley and Games, through Fletcher, Forbes and Gill, to Brody, Saville and Garrett.

This survey of the next wave of the UK's graphics innovators may provide some clues as to the identity of future trendsetters, but Britain's graphic world may not yet be quite ready to fall obediently into line.

Graphic design in the UK is in a state of flux, both stylistically and systemically. A scan through these pages will reveal many alternate directions for the dominant style of tomorrow. Perhaps the tactility and crafts-based work of, say, Lizzie Finn may herald an analogue revolt against the all-powerful Mac, reflecting a rejection of the primacy of technology gaining ground in the wider world? Or will the style be software-driven, linked perhaps to the capabilities of the latest version of Flash, with print graphics being mere screenshots of their web-based source? Certainly, the likes of Digit and Rom and Son are adding some much-needed heart and soul to interactive work. But we should also consider who the possible consumers of this new style are likely to be, for they may well help forge its construction.

Traditionally, there have been three fields that have been the prime sponsors of innovation in graphic design:

publishing, music and fashion. Think of the great stylistic leaders of graphic design in the last 30 years and all of them will have worked in one or more of these areas.

Publishing remains a fertile area for innovation. Magazine design is still reaping the benefits of the desktop publishing revolution, which allowed for a new wave of independent, adventurous titles that played with the form and function of the periodical. The latest manifestation of this opportunity is the bi-annual – lavish, visually led, high cover-price publications, usually aimed at the fashion market and advertisers, that include such titles as **Pop**, **The Fashion** and **Another Magazine**. Book design, too, remains a fruitful area for graphic expression. Print is far from dead.

In fashion and music, however, the picture is less rosy. Even though it is seen as a very desirable area in which to work, the graphic designer's role is peripheral to the business of fashion. Photography remains the dominant means of the communication of ideas here and is enjoying something of a golden age. Recently, such experienced hands as Peter Saville have noted a growing interest in what graphic design can offer high-fashion clients, particularly in terms of the mise en page, the bringing together of photography, type and graphic elements. Structurally, however, the high-fashion business is changing towards a situation that may not be as conducive to innovation. Two huge conglomerates now dominate: LVMH and PPR (owners of the Gucci Group), with Prada, thanks to the acquisition of Fendi, Jil Sander and Helmut Lang, fast coming up on the rails. Big groups traditionally breed conservatism. Add an economic downturn, which has hit fashion very hard, and you have a recipe for sticking to the tried and trusted: already Prada has seemingly abandoned its policy of using young photographers in favour of big names. If fashion is to remain a patron of innovative graphic designers, the evidence suggests it will only be the small, young companies, not the established brands.

Similarly in music, changes in the industry have put a once-fertile area of graphic expression under threat. Like fashion, there has been a pattern of mergers and acquisitions, resulting in the domination of a few big players. Sleeve artwork budgets have been shrinking for years, as marketing departments turn to other areas – promos, websites and so on. Single sales have plummeted. Pressure from retailers has resulted in restrictions being imposed on designers: the band name, for example, must not be in such a position that it may be obscured by the price sticker, which, stores dictate, always goes in the same place. The only bright spot has been the growth of "faceless" dance acts on smaller labels, such as Warp and Skam, where there is no pressure to put a photograph of the artists on the cover and far more scope for innovation.

Perhaps we need another white knight to step forward as a patron of the new, now that the traditional consumers of fresh talent and ideas can no longer be relied upon: niche retailers perhaps, or the explosion of new television channels? TV would certainly provide an outlet for one of the more striking developments of recent years: the shift into motion graphics.

Improved desktop computing power and software have opened up a new dimension to graphic designers, for whom the lure of seeing their work move has proved difficult to resist. Hence we have a new genre of design and designer – moving image work made by the graphic film-maker. Events such as onedotzero and Resfest showcase the work of this new breed that includes the likes of Johnny Hardstaff and Richard Fenwick. Just as digital cameras have allowed designers to take their own photographs and create their own illustrations, the digital video camera is now also standard studio equipment.

There is a buzz around the motion graphics scene right now, which suggests that if there is to be a new design superstar emerging in the next couple of years – a Carson or a Brody – then he or, let's hope, she will come from this area. Not so long ago, the Web would have seemed the natural place to look for a new hero, but the dot.com crash has, for the moment at least, shifted the focus towards measurable effectiveness and usability and away from experimentation. Which is not to deny that interactive design will exert an

influence on the graphics scene, although it may be as much about attitude as style. New media designers have a different mind set to their print cousins. The Web, being built on principles of the free and open exchange of information (the so-called "open source culture") encourages activism that rails against the corporate world. As an industry, design rather forgot its political and social responsibilities after the 1980s, but the younger wave are showing signs of rediscovering a moral imperative, thanks in part to having come in contact with this culture. An example is the New Media Underground Festival, a group of designers who, outraged at the high prices being charged by conferences such as Flash Forward, are attempting to organize their own alternative, not-for-profit events to share information and ideas. Throw in the relaunch of Ken Garland's **First Things First** manifesto, Naomi Klein's **No Logo** book and the anti-WTO protests, and many designers have begun to question their role as servants of corporate power.

The design community is becoming as diverse as the work that it produces, from huge corporate brand identity projects to one-man font foundries, from FMCG packaging to the increasing number of designers making work for sale in galleries. One of the challenges in putting together this book was to represent that diversity without imposing arbitrary categories on contributors: they defy such pigeonholing. Instead, we hope you enjoy the clash of method and style between, say, A2-Graphics, Shynola and Steff Plaetz.

This plurality makes the imposition of a new dominant style in the future less likely than in the past. Perhaps it is a sign of increased confidence among designers, rather like the way that youth culture appears to have abandoned the tribalism of the 1980s. It is no longer necessary to belong to one camp or another, to follow one true guru to the exclusion of all others. There will still be stars, but could this be the end of the designism?

PATRICK BURGOYNE

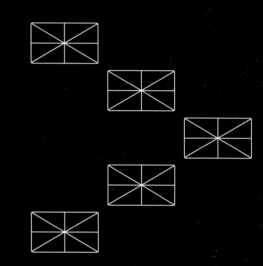

AVENY-T FREDERIKSBERG ALLÉ 102 T +45 7020 1031 W WWW.AVENY-T.DK
DK-1820 FREDERIKSBERG C F +45 3323 3785 E INFO@AVENY-T.DK

AVENY-T

THE TEST TRUE OF A CITY'S IS NOT ITS COMMERCE VITALITY BUT ITS ARTS

ALBERT EINSTEIN

Title Aveny-T Visual Language Description Promotional house style for new theatre in Copenhagen, Denmark Medium Print Date 2001

TYPOGRAPHY/ HENRIK KUBEL A2-GRAPHICS/SW/HK

BUCKINGHAMSHIRE CHILTERNS
UNIVERSITY COLLEGE
E2 DEPARTMENT OF 2 DIMENSIONAL DESIGN
BA (HONS) GRAPHIC DESIGN & ADVERTISING
SEMESTER 1 2001/ 1 ELECTIVE 03

DESIGN/ RE-LAUNCH/ RE-PACK
THE BEATLES' SGT. PEPPER'S LONELY
HEARTS CLUB BAND

THE FORMAT IS FREE BUT MUST INCLUDE
THE DESIGN OF A COMPACT DISC

FINAL DESIGN MUST BE BACKED UP
BY RESEARCH

LIST OF SONGS TO BE INCLUDED
SIDE 01
SGT. PEPPER'S LONELY HEARTS CLUB BAND
A LITTLE HELP FROM MY FRIENDS
LUCY IN THE SKY WITH DIAMONDS
GETTING BETTER
FIXING A HOLE
SHE'S LEAVING HOME
BEING FOR THE BENEFIT OF MR. KITE!

SIDE 02
WITHIN YOU WITHOUT YOU
WHEN I'M SIXTY-FOUR
LOVELY RITA
GOOD MORNING, GOOD MORNING
SGT. PEPPER'S LONELY HEARTS CLUB BAND (REPRISE)
A DAY IN THE LIFE

STUDENTS TO ATTEND:
JAMILLA CHAUDHRY
EMILY CONWAY
JON-PAUL DALY
TOM DELEE

CHRIS GLOSTER
NEIL HARRIS
ELLEN HEHIR
BACH-MAI HO
GEMMA KENWARD

KRISTIAN LABAK
ANNE-MARIE OWRAM
OLIVIER RABENSCHLAG
SIMON SCOTT
LOUISE SHEARER

Title: Typography Workshop: Re-design The Beatles' Sgt Pepper's Lonely Hearts Club Band   Description: One of a series of posters outlining typographic courses at Buckingham University College   Medium: Print   Date: 2000-2001

Title: www.fontyoufonts.com   Description: Logo for online type foundry   Medium: Web   Date: 2000

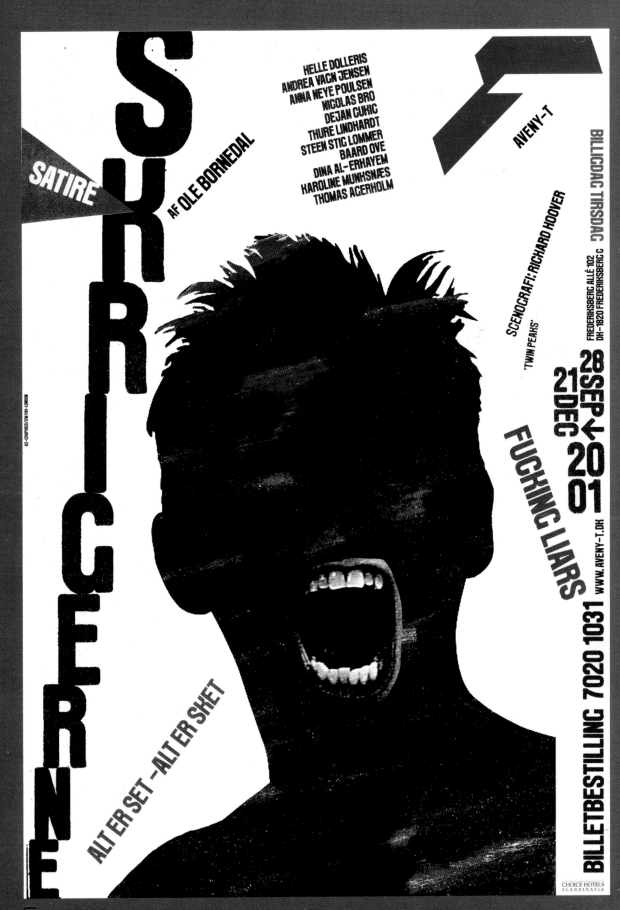

Title: Skrigerne 'The Screamers' Description: Promotional poster for Aveny-T theatre, Copenhagen, Denmark Medium: Print Date: 2001

46 bittersweet

35 tranquil

31 prosperity

Title: The Interactive Colouring Book   Description: Digital interpretation of "painting by numbers"   Media: CD-ROM and touch-screen version   Date: 2000

AIRSIDE

Title: Battle Royale Description: Promotional T-shirts for the Japanese feature film Battle Royale Medium: Textile print Date: 2001

23RD FLOOR

23RD FLOOR

please select ic

games   music   phone food

icon constructor interface

HERE, WITH THIS MIGHTY TOOL, at last you can sculpt at your leisure the logo that your imagination craves and your ego deserves. Hewn from the living pixel, create a monument to your individuality that will shine like a beacon for all to admire. And if you don't like it – throw it away and start again!

COMING SOON !

make your dream a reality

Title: 23rd Floor   Description: Music and phone games website   Medium: Web   Date: 2001

monster music motherload

A vast array of minstrels from far and wide gather here in our virtual backstage complex, waiting eagerly to dance and sing their hour upon the stage for your delectation and delight. The briskest beats, the sweetest melodies, the most vivacious vocals, all yours at the touch of a button.

If music be the food of love - phone on!

You'll need Realplayer to hear the tunes - then click on a pattern.

Let the music play

pop

The biggest movers, breakers and shakers in the wonderful world of pop. Today's hits, tomorrow's hi-fliers

Interview: Shaggy

Interview: Elbow

Interview: Turin Brakes

Interview: Scene In...Notting Hill Carnival

Pop Gossip: Lip Service

dance

Two hours of essential new music across the dance spectrum; UK Garage and Disco through to Progressive House in the Mix.

Interview: Roots Manuva

Interview: I-Monster

Kingsland Road / East

Title: Panorama: Kingsland Road, Hackney   Description: Folding and detachable panoramic guide of the historic Kingsland Road for The Building Exploratory   Medium: Print
Date: 2001   Photography: Otmar Dressel, Palmira Alloggia, Lisa Rigg, Daniel Cope Stephens and Polly Richards

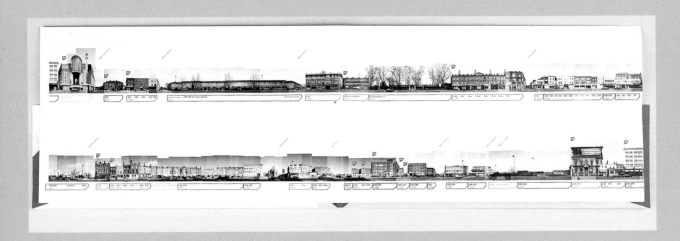

Panorama-
Kingsland Road Hackney London

One of the oldest roads in Britain runs through Hackney. Kingsland Road is a 2,000 year old Roman road and has been home to manufacturers, traders and craftspeople for centuries. On this road between Shoreditch and Dalston, cabinet makers, saddlers and glass makers once worked alongside ostrich feather cleaners, confectioners and fancy brush manufacturers. Today people continue to come to Kingsland Road for its great variety of family-run and independent shops, businesses and eateries, as well as its religious and cultural venues.

The national importance of this road has recently been recognised by English Heritage, who made it a conservation area in 1993.

This guide has been commissioned by the Kingsland Conservation Area Partnership to celebrate and publicise its new status. The guide reproduces in miniature a photographic panorama of the road, and provides information about its fascinating buildings and history.

The Building Exploratory is a Hackney-based centre that explores the local built environment through a hands-on exhibition and educational activities in the community.

Panorama·
- *Kingsland Road* / Hackney London

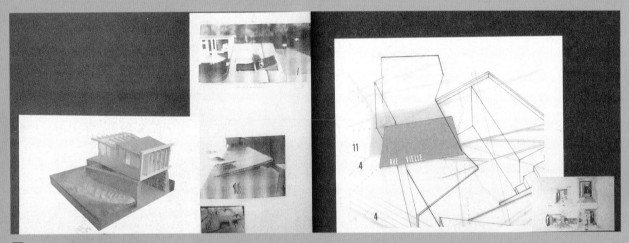

Title: Exposure   Description: Catalogue for Kingston University Design Degree and Diploma Shows   Medium: Print   Date: 2001

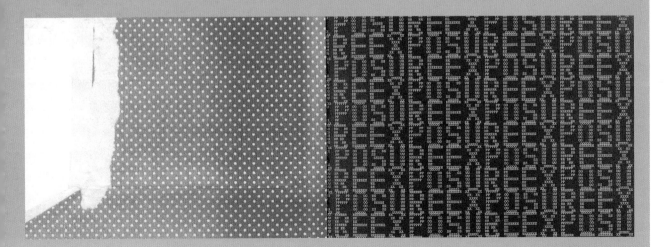

EXPOSURE

KINGSTON UNIVERSITY

DESIGN DEGREE & DIPLOMA SHOWS 2001

13, 14, 15 June   10am - 9pm daily
Friends & Family Day   16 June   10am - 4pm

Architecture / Landscape Architecture / Art +
Design History / Fashion / Fine Art / Foundat
Graphic Design / Illustration / HND Graphic De
Music / Photography / Product + Furniture Des
Interior Design / Surveying

Kingston University   T +44 (0)20 8547 886
Faculty of Design   F +44 (0)20 8547 706
Knights Park   E c.shepherdson@king
Kingston upon Thames
Surrey KT1 2QJ   www.kingston.ac.uk

Design automatic • Paul Greece
Printed by RAN Press
Printed on 150gsm Consort Royal Brilliance by Donside

Title: Exposure   Description: Poster for Kingston University Design Degree and Diploma Shows   Medium: Print   Date: 2001   Designed with Paul Greeno

Communication Art and Design

Royal College of Art
Work in Progress Exhibition 2000

Galleries Open:
10am–6pm
Monday–Saturday

Kensington Gore
London, SW7 2EU

First Year Students
17–26 January
Entrance Gallery

Second Year Students
12–26 January
Upper Gulbenkian Gallery

Title: Work in Progress Exhibition   Description: Poster design for the RCA show Work in Progress   Medium: Silk-screen print   Date: 2000   Designed with Simon Lamb

Title: Village Fete at the V&A   Description: Promotional poster for the two-day design event, held in the Pirelli Gardens at the V&A, London   Medium: Lithography print   Date: 2001   Designed with John Hares

WOW! PARTY IS NICE TIME.
ALL YOU FELLOWS LEARNING BRIGHT
IDEAS OLD AND YOUNG SPRITE,
LETS BE GOOD FRIENDS. EXCITING!
JUMP AND SHOUT! COME AND
LOVE YOUR ENEMY. BE MAN AND
WOMAN. LISTEN UP! SMASH SOUND
HITS. JUICE! MILK! BEER! TASTY
SNACKS! LETS QUAFF! YEAH,
PRICE IS NICE MICE. CHEER UP NICE
GUY — ITS GONNA BE OK, YOU WIN
DRINK! DON'T BE DUMMY, LOVE TO
COMPETE FOOTBALL? VERY VERY
THANKS WITH MY TEARS.

1ST AND 2ND YEAR
COMMUNICATIONS PARTY
RCA CAFÉ
TUESDAY 7 DECEMBER
6.00PM START
£3 ENTRANCE AND BEER
TABLE FOOTBALL COMPETITION
SIGN-UP SHEET LOCATED ON
GRAPHICS NOTICEBOARD

Title: Communication Art and Design   Description: Gold and fluorescent-yellow poster for RCA party   Medium: Print   Date: 2000   Designed with Sean Murphy

Anatomy Course

Drawing Studio
Spring Term 1999

Royal College of Art

Thursday 22 January
11.00am–12.30pm
Drawing Studio: Introduction.
Course introduction by Deanna Petherbridge.
Sarah Simblet: 20 minute presentation on her current
drawings and research.
Bridget Landon: 20 minute presentation on studying
human dissection.
Questions and registration for the course.

Thursday 29 January
11.00am–12.30pm
The Head and Neck.
Bridget Landon lecture: "Talking, Laughing,
Swallowing," in the Drawing Studio.

1.45am–4.45pm
Drawing from dissection with Bridget Landon at the
Anatomy Theatre, University College, London.

Tuesday 3 February
10.00am–5.00pm
Seeing Structure.
Drawing Studio session all day with Sarah Simblet.

Thursday 5 February
10.00am–4.45pm
Visit to the Hunterian and Wellcome Museums at the
Royal College of Surgeons, Lincolns Inn Field.
Meet at the entrance 10am, bring drawing materials,
(no cameras).
Introduction by Sarah Simblet.
Drawing in museums all day.

Thursday 12 February
11.00am–12.30pm
The Axial Skeleton.
Bridget Landon lecture: "The Fulcrum of Diversity,"
in the Drawing Studio.

1.45pm–4.45pm
Demonstration and drawing from dissection with
Bridget Landon at the Dissecting Room, University
College, London.

Monday 16 February
10.00am–5.00pm
Mapping the Torso.
Drawing Studio session all day with Sarah Simblet.

Thursday 19 February
11.00am–12.30pm
The Limbs.
Bridget Landon lecture: "The Limbs of the Body,"
in the Drawing Studio.

1.45pm–4.45pm
Demonstration and drawing from dissection with
Bridget Landon at the Dissecting Room, University
College, London.

Tuesday 24 February
10.00am–5.00pm
Walruses and Mice.
Drawing Studio: Comparative anatomy.
Drawing session all day with Steve Dilworth.

Wednesday 25 February
10.00am–5.00pm
Walruses and Mice.
Drawing Studio: Comparative anatomy.
Drawing session all day with Steve Dilworth.

Thursday 26 February
10.00am–12.30pm
1.45pm–4.45pm
Unethical uses of Anatomy.
Drawing Studio session all day with Eleanor Crook
including a slide talk on her work.

Thursday 5 March
11.00am–12.30pm
Balance and Gait.
Bridget Landon lecture: "Balance and Gait," in the
Drawing Studio.

1.45pm–4.45pm
Demonstration and drawing from dissection with
Bridget Landon at the Dissecting Room, University
College, London.

Thursday 12 March
10.00am–12.30pm
La Specola.
Sarah Simblet lecture: "La Specola," in the
Drawing Studio.

1.45pm–4.45pm
Visit to the Science Museum to draw from
Italian waxes.

Thursday 19 March
11.00am–12.30pm
1.45pm–4.45pm
Extremities: A Study of Hands and Feet.
Bridget Landon lecture: "Touching Ground," at the
Dissecting Room, University College, London.

Thursday 26 March
10.00am–5.00pm
Drawing Studio session all day with Sarah Simblet.

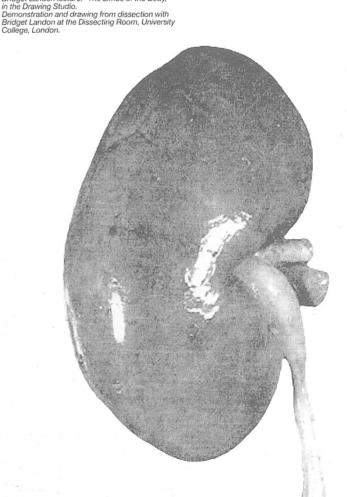

Design: Simon Lamb/Nicholas Barba

Title: RCA Anatomy Course   Description: In-house publicity poster for RCA drawing studio   Medium: Silk-screen print   Date: 2000   Designed with Simon Lamb

Title: Web 3d Art   Description: Poster and publicity material for an exhibition exploring
3D design on the web, at the ICA, London   Medium: Print   Date: 2002

Title: Journey into Lost Futurism   Description: A photographic book investigating and reinventing the effect of modernist environments, authored, photographed and designed by Bark   Medium: Print   Date: 2001

re-assembled

SERIES: FORWARD FUTURISM

ELEVATION: REINVENTION

0→

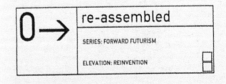

0→ re-assembled

SERIES: FORWARD FUTURISM

ELEVATION: REINVENTION

skywards

LOST FUTURISM

Title: Astro Cuntry Description: A colony of B-bots are unleashed upon a rural community
Medium: Digital montage Date: 2002 Photography and design: Matt Watkins

Title: BrumPeeps   Description: A montage of Lucy McLauchlan's illustration and Beat 13 iconography, reflecting the optimism of Birmingham's inhabitants about the city's changing landscape   Medium: Digital montage
Date: 2002   Photography and design: Matt Watkins

Title: 26.2   Description: Time Out magazine supplement for the London Marathon, sponsored by Adidas   Medium: Print   Date: 2001

Title: London Marathon Road Signs   Description: Staged road signs as part of the Adidas London Marathon advertising campaign, photographed for Time Out magazine supplement   Medium: Print   Date: 2001
Photography: Darren Regnier

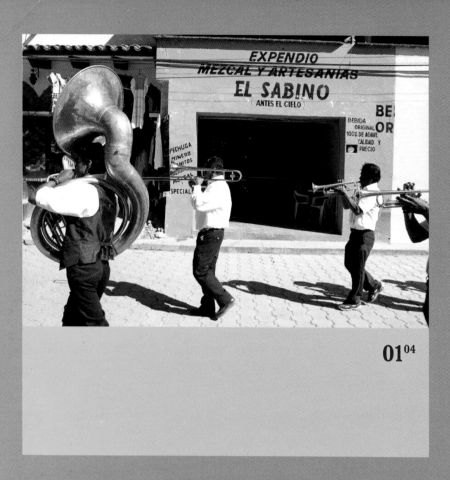

01⁰⁴

Title: Panoptica   Description: 10" Series sleeve designs for Certificate 18 Records
Medium: Print   Date: 2001   Photographer: Gemma Booth

Title: Pilote: Do It Now Man   Description: CD and album cover for Pilote on Certificate 18 Records   Medium: Print   Date: 2001

The Club   ICA The Mall London SW1Y 5AH 15:11:2000
19.00-21.00   RSVP; sarad@ica.org.uk T: 020 7372 0240
CAP GEMINI ERNST&YOUNG   NESTA   CHANNEL 4   THE ARTS COUNCIL   GOLDSMITHS COLLEGE   ICA

Title: The Club ICA   Description: Poster and invitation publicizing The Club at the ICA   Medium: Print   Date: 2000

Broken glass everywhere People pissing on the stairs, you know they just don't care I can't take the smell, I can't take the noise Got no money to move out, I guess I got no choice Rats in the front room, roaches in the back Junkie's in the alley with a baseball bat I tried to get away, but I couldn't get far Cause the man with the tow-truck repossessed my car Don't push me, cause I'm close to the edge I'm trying not to loose my head It's like a jungle sometimes, it makes me wonder How I keep from going under Standing on the front stoop, hangin' out the window Watching all the cars go by, roaring as the breezes blow Crazy lady, livin' in a bag Eating out of garbage piles, used to be a fag-hag Search and test a tango, skips the life and then go To search a prince to see the last of senses Down at the peepshow, watching all the creeps So she can tell the stories to the girls back home She went to the city and got so so so ditty She had to get a pimp, she couldn't make it on her own Don't push me, cause I'm close to the edge I'm trying not to loose my head It's like a jungle sometimes, it makes me wonder How I keep from going under Standing on the front stoop, ha It's like a jungle sometimes, it makes me wonder How I keep from goin' under My brother's doing fast on my mother's T.V. Says she watches to much, is just not healthy All my children in the daytime, Dallas at night Can't even see the game or the Sugar Ray fight Bill collectors they ring my phone And scare my wife when I'm not home Got a bum education, double-digit inflation Can't take the train to the job, there's a strike at the station Me on King Kong standin' on my back Can't stop to turn around, broke my sacroiliac Midrange, migrained, cancered membrane Sometimes I think I'm going insane, I swear I might hijack a plane! Don't push me, cause I'm close to the edge I'm trying not to loose my head It's like a jungle sometimes, it makes me wonder How I keep from going under Standing on the front stoop, ha My son said daddy I don't wanna go to school Cause the teacher's a jerk, he must think I'm a fool And all the kids smoke reefer, I think it'd be cheaper If I just got a job, learned to be a street sweeper I dance to the beat, shuffle my feet Wear a shirt and tie and run with the creeps Cause it's all about money, ain't a damn thing funny You got to have a con in this land of milk and honey They push that girl in front of a train Took her to a doctor, sowed the arm on again Stabbed that man, right in his heart Gave him a transplant before a brand new start I can't walk through the park, cause it's crazy after the dark Keep my hand on the gun, cause they got me on the run I feel like an outlaw, broke my last fast jaw Hear them say you want some more, livin' on a seasaw Don't push me, cause I'm close to the edge I'm trying not to loose my head It's like a jungle sometimes, it makes me wonder How I keep from going under Standing on the front stoop, ha A child was born, wih no state of mind Blind to the ways of mankind Got a smile on you with these burning tooth Cause only god knows what you go through You grow in the ghetto, living second rate And your eyes will sing a song of deep hate The places you play and where you stay Looks like one great big alley way You'll admire all the numberbook takers Dogpitchers, pushers and the big money makers Driving big cars, spending twenties and tens And you wanna grow up to be just like them Smuygglers, scrambles, burglars, gamblers Pickpockets, peddlers and even pan-handlers You say I'm cool, I'm no fool But then you wind up dropping out of highschool Now you're unemployed, all null 'n' void Walking around like you're pretty boy Floyd Turned stickup kid, look what you done did Got send up for a eight year bid Now your man is took and you're a Maytag Spend the next two years as an undercover fag Being used and abused, and served like hell Till one day you was find hung dead in a cell It was plain to see that your life was lost You was cold and your body swung back and forth But now your eyes sing the sad sad song Of how you lived so fast and died so young Don't push me, cause I'm close to the edge I'm trying not to loose my head It's likè a jungle sometimes, it makes me wonder How I keep from going under

Rapping paper © bump 2001   Artist: Grandmaster Melle Mel and Duke Bootee   Album: The Sugar Hill Records Story: Disc ThreeTitle: The Message

Title: Rapping Paper   Description: Gift wrapping paper for the ICA shop   Medium: Print   Date: 2001

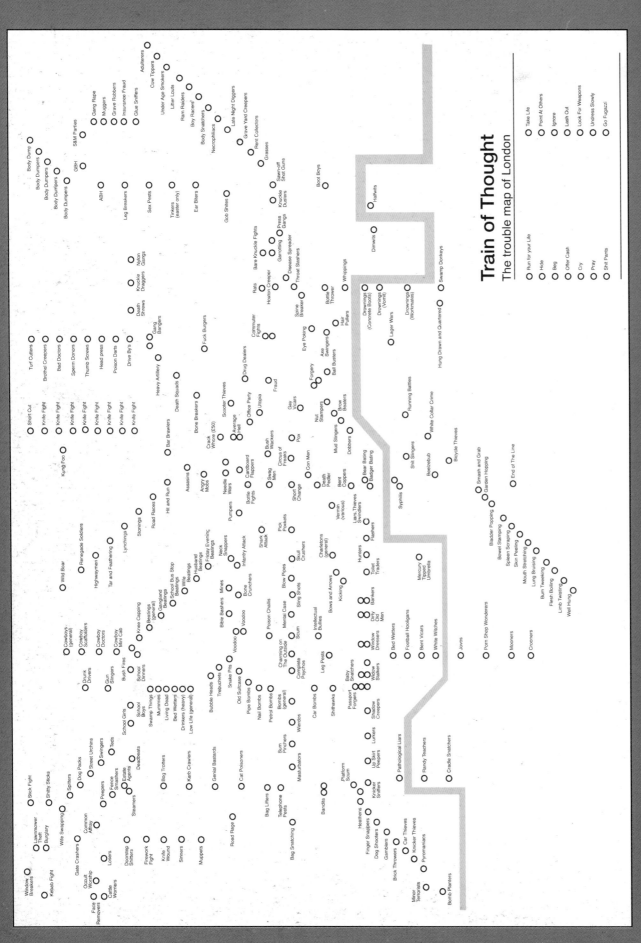

Train of Thought
The trouble map of London

- Run for your Life
- Hide
- Beg
- Offer Cash
- Cry
- Pray
- Shit Pants

- Take Life
- Point At Others
- Ignore
- Lash Out
- Look For Weapons
- Undress Slowly
- Go Fugazzi

Title: Train of Thought Description: Map made for the JAM exhibition at The Barbican Medium: Print Date: 2001

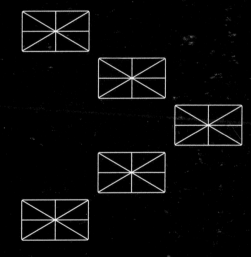

Title: Valentine's Day at Nutta's House   Description: Frame from the cartoon strip based on readers' problems, featured in the teenage fashion magazine J17   Medium: Print   Date: 2001-present

DAVID BURNS

Title: The Scene Queens   Description: Characters from the monthly cartoon strip featured in J17 magazine
Medium: Print   Date: 2001-present

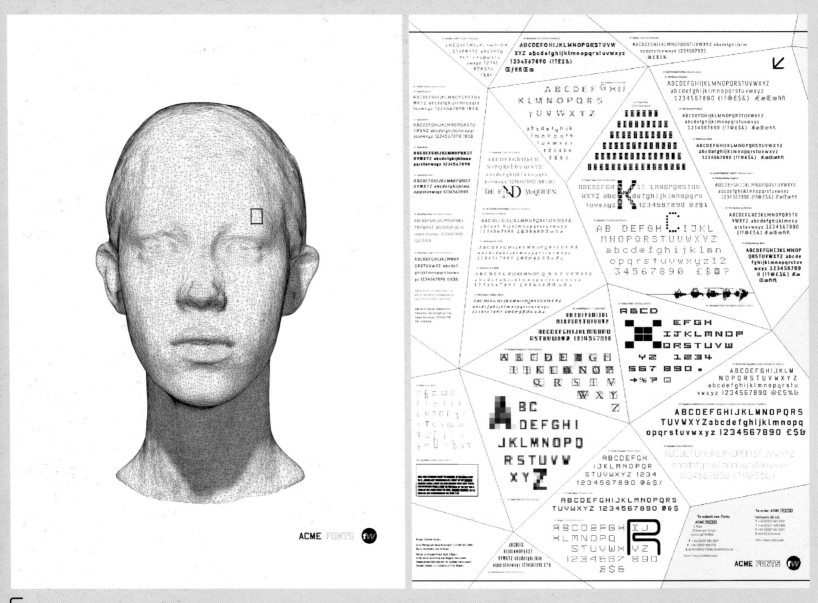

Title: Typeface   Description: Poster for type foundry Acme Fonts   Medium: Print   Date: 2000   Photography: Sølve Sundsbø

ACME FONTS

Title: Archi-typographic   Description: Poster for the type foundry Acme Fonts   Medium: Print   Date: 2001

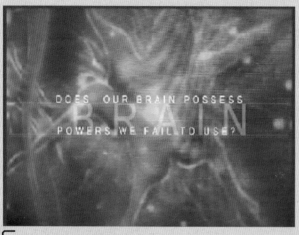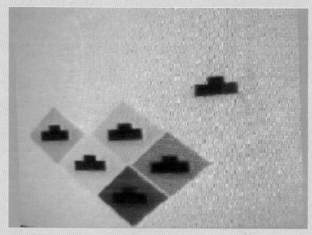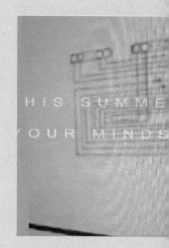

� Title: ai   Description: Animated cinema teaser submitted for competition to Ridley Scott Associates   Medium: Video   Date: 2000

⎘ Title: Dancing in my Head   Description: Three-minute personal project using a track by Blur   Medium: Video   Date: 2000

⎘ Title: Life Style Obsession   Description: Shortlisted animated film for Digitalent, in association with Channel 4 and Tango   Medium: Video   Date: 2001

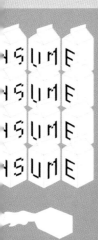

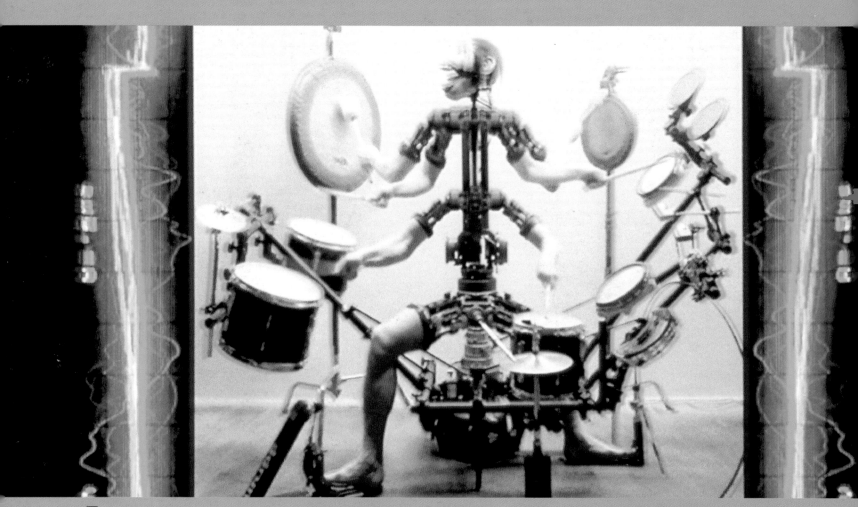

Title: Monkey Drummer   Description: two-minute film for exhibition   Medium: 35mm film transferred onto DVD   Date: 2000-2001

CHRIS CUNNINGHAM

Title: Mental Wealth   Description: Advert for Playstation 2   Medium: Mini DV   Date: 1998   Courtesy of RSA/BlackDog and Playstation

Title: Flex Description: Stills from 12-minute film shown in exhibition Medium: 35mm film transferred onto DVD video Date: 2000-2001

CHRIS CUNNINGHAM

#012   CHRIS CUNNINGHAM

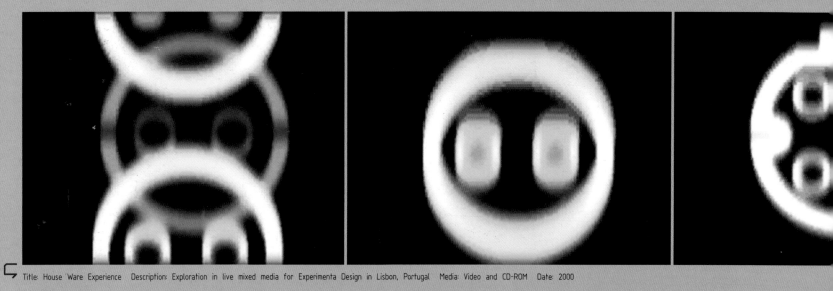

Title: House 'Ware Experience   Description: Exploration in live mixed media for Experimenta Design in Lisbon, Portugal   Media: Video and CD-ROM   Date: 2000

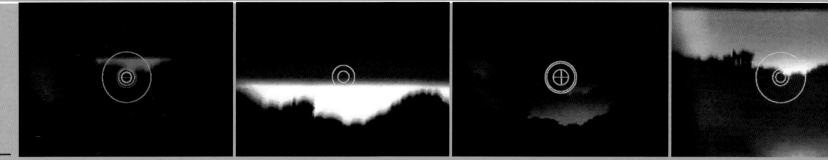

Title: Intro. Movie   Description: Introductory movie for D-Fuse promotional CD   Medium: Video and CD-ROM   Date: 2001

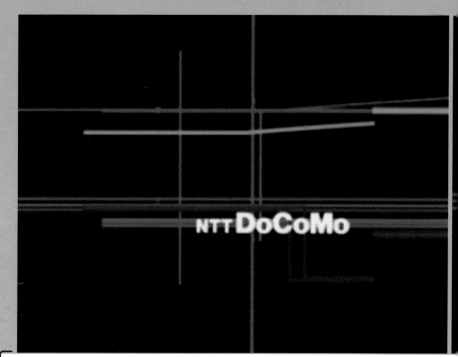

Title: NTT DoCoMo   Description: Motion-graphic sequence for corporate logo for the Japanese Telecommunications company NTT DoCoMo   Medium: Video and CD-ROM   Date: 2001   Designed with Raw Paw

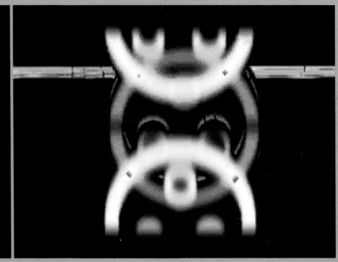

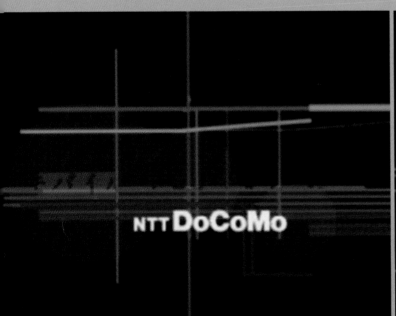

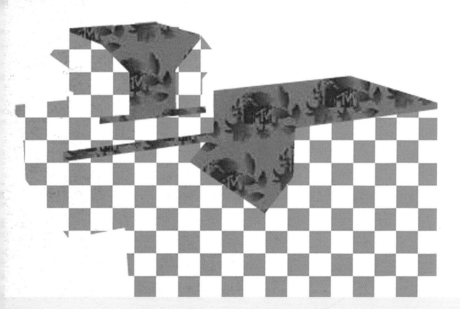

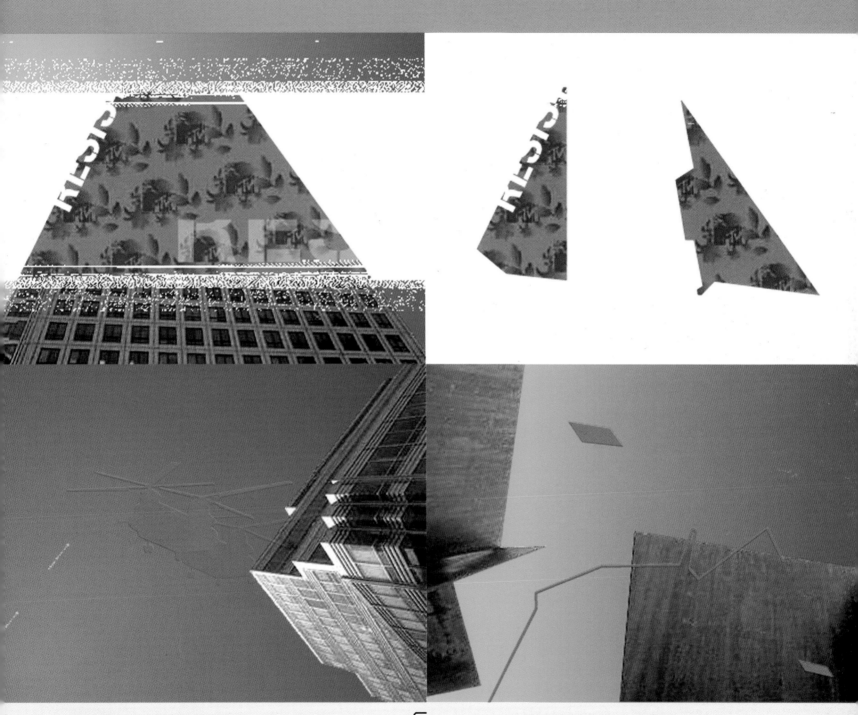

Title: MTV Source   Description: 20-second email attachment animation and dedicated microsite
Medium: Flash animation   Date: 2001   Photography and design: Merlin Nation

Title: MTV Dance Channel Idents   Description: Dance-programming idents with different colours for each zone and time of broadcast   Medium: Video   Date: 2001

DRAUGHT ASSOCIATES

Title: Slave   Description: Detail from title sequence of Style magazine programme
on Channel 4   Medium: Video   Date: 2000

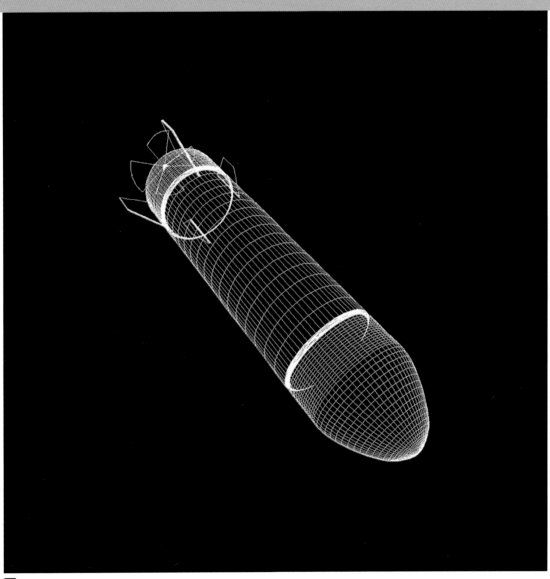

Title: Auto Sub   Description: Detail of signage for the British Pavilion at Lisbon Expo on the theme of "Oceans"   Medium: Audio-visual   Date: 1998

DRAUGHT ASSOCIATES

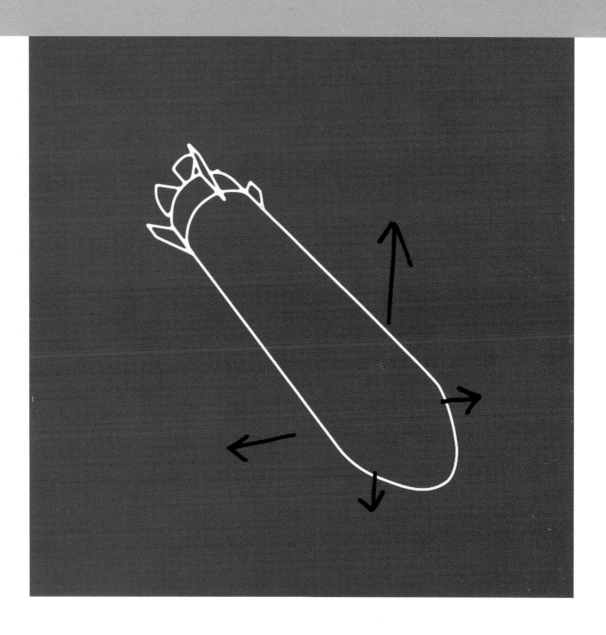

Title: Reality and Myth in a Land of Consultants Description: Design for page incorporating logo produced for Kohkoku magazine (Japanese contemporary culture) Medium: Print Date: 2001

Title: Fat Town   Description: Animation involving the assembly of a townscape using iconic urban structures and elements   Medium: Web   Date: 2001

FAT

Title: RND#06: Underworld   Description: Short film from the art project Random Number, an on-going series of 100 short films   Medium: Digital film   Date: 2000

Title: RND#88: End Users   Description: Short film from the Random Number series   Medium: Digital film   Date: 2000

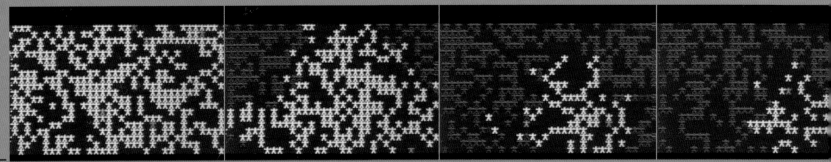

Title: RND#67: Virus   Description: Short film from the Random Number series   Medium: Digital film   Date: 2000

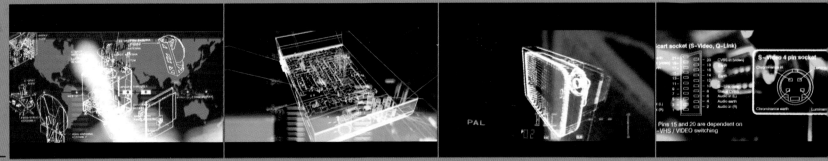

Title: RND#23: Content Provider   Description: Short film from the Random Number series   Medium: Digital film   Date: 2001   Designed with David Park, Dorian Thomas, Andrew Morley,
Sarah Ramsden, Dan Capstick and Adam Fox

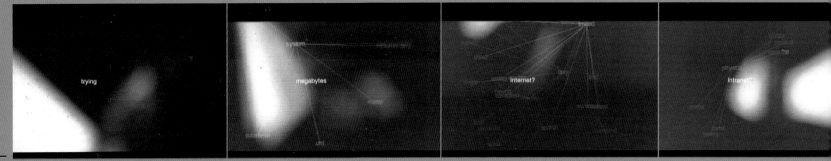

Title: RND#91: 51st State   Description: Short film from the Random Number series   Medium: Digital film   Date: 2000

017

RICHARD FENWICK

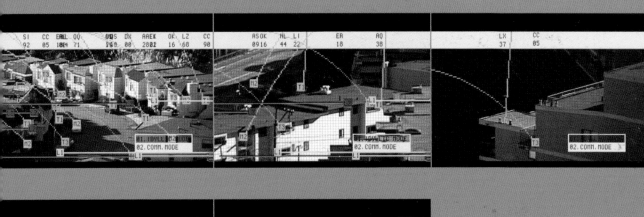

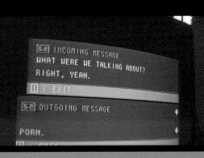

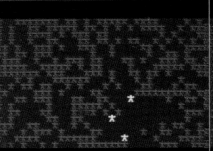
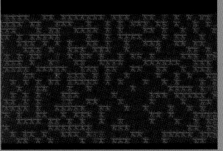

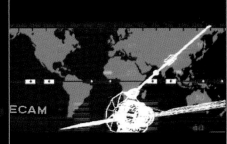

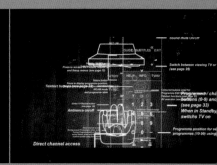

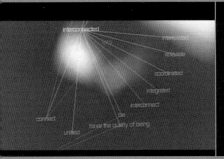
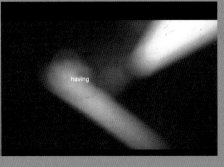

Title: Lettering for Relax style magazine, Tokyo Description: Double-page opening spread with embroidered lettering for a feature on Silas, a UK clothing company Medium: Print Date: 2001

018

LIZZIE FINN

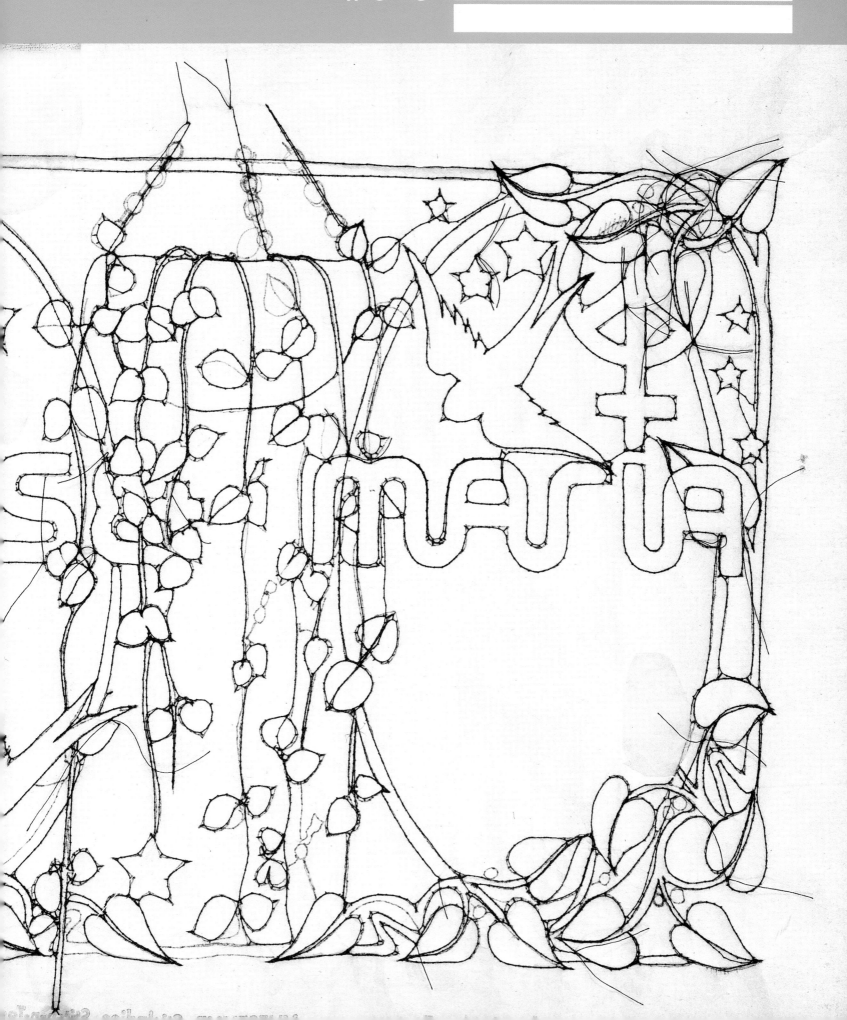

Title: Trans-Form, Trans-It, Trans-Port Description: Photograph for a conceptual project, presenting observations of tower cranes Media: Print, Web and CD-ROM Date: 2001

FL@33

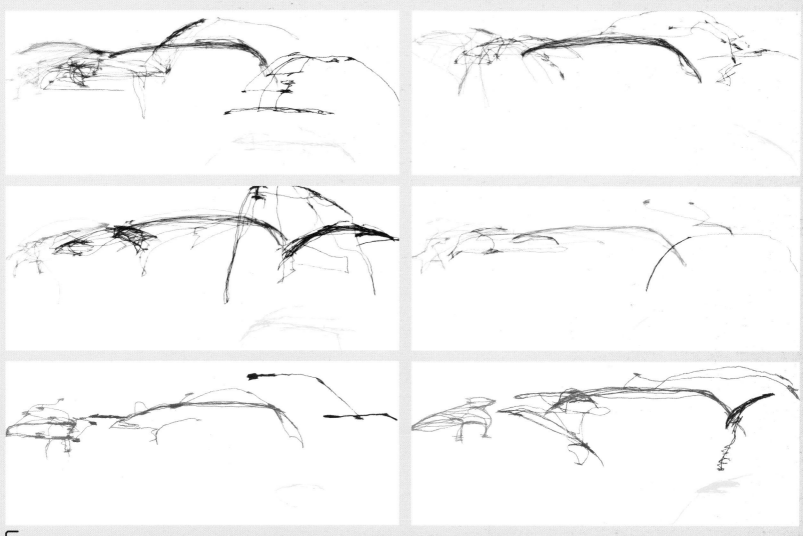

⊊ Title: Crane Movements   Description: Colour-coded observation of tower cranes for a double-page spread in Trans-Form magazine   Medium: Print   Date: 2001

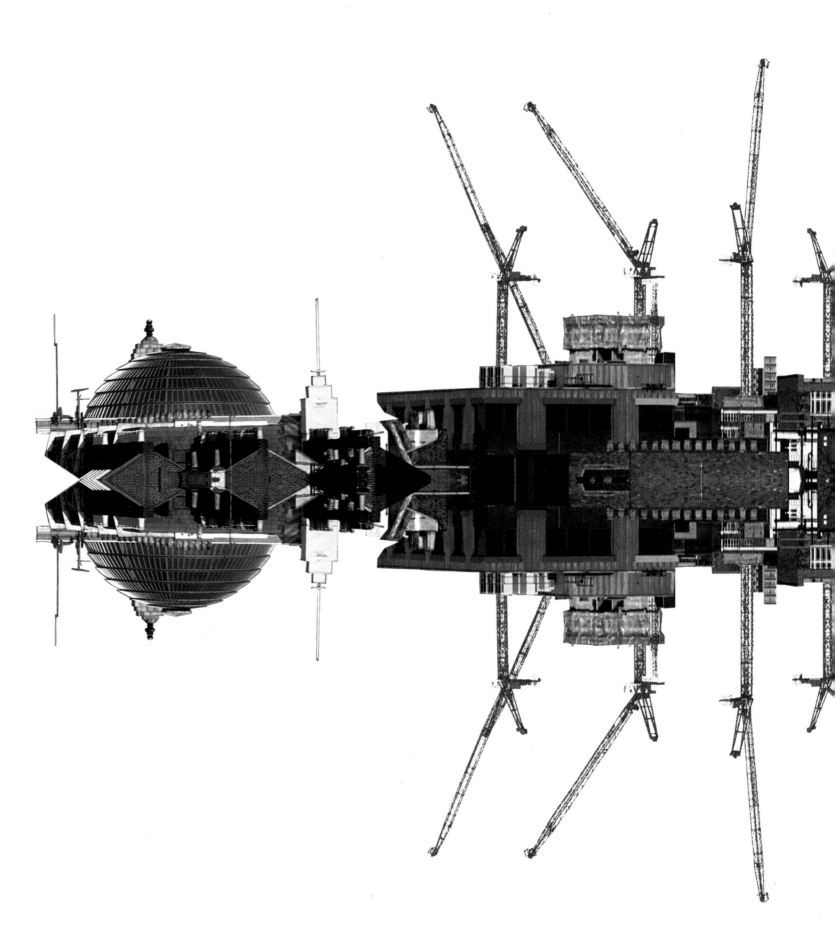

Title: Trans-Form   Description: Double-page spread from the conceptual project Trans-Form   Medium: Print   Date: 2001

FL@33

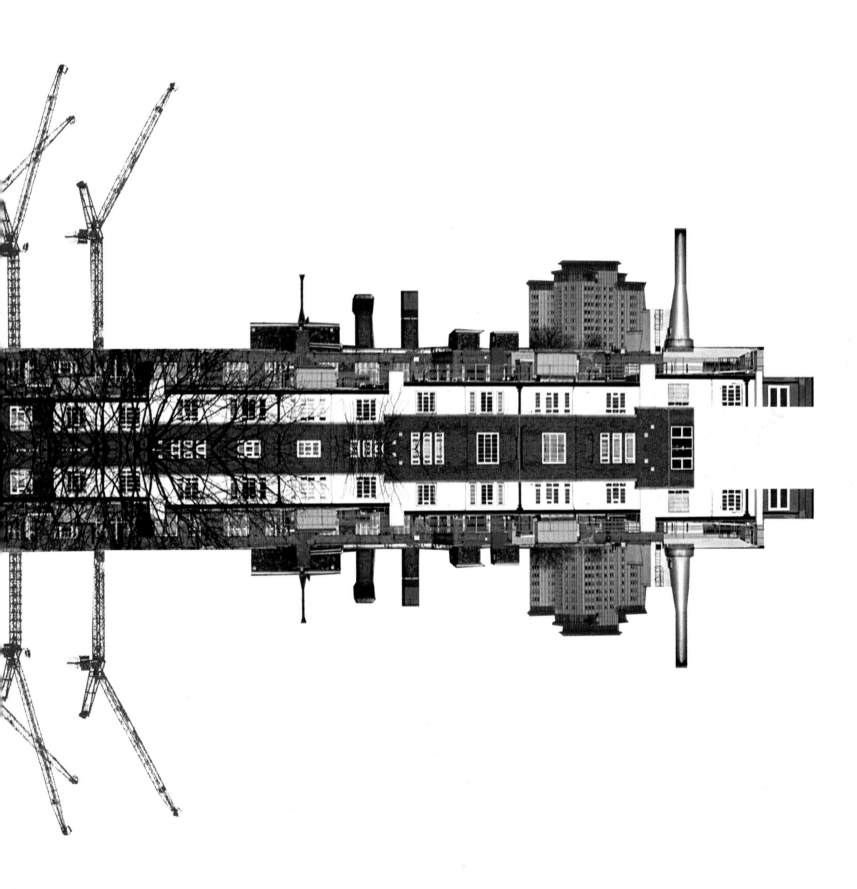

Title: 250g Peach   Description: Collaborative email project between UK and Japan for exhibition in Japan
Media: Mixed including EPS drawing, laser prints, pencil and acrylic paint   Date: 2001
Design: Lee Basford/Momoko Hayashi

Title: Man Two   Description: Part of a collaborative email project   Media: Mixed including EPS drawing,
laser prints, pencil and acrylic paint   Date: 2001   Design: Lee Basford/Momoko Hayashi

FLUID

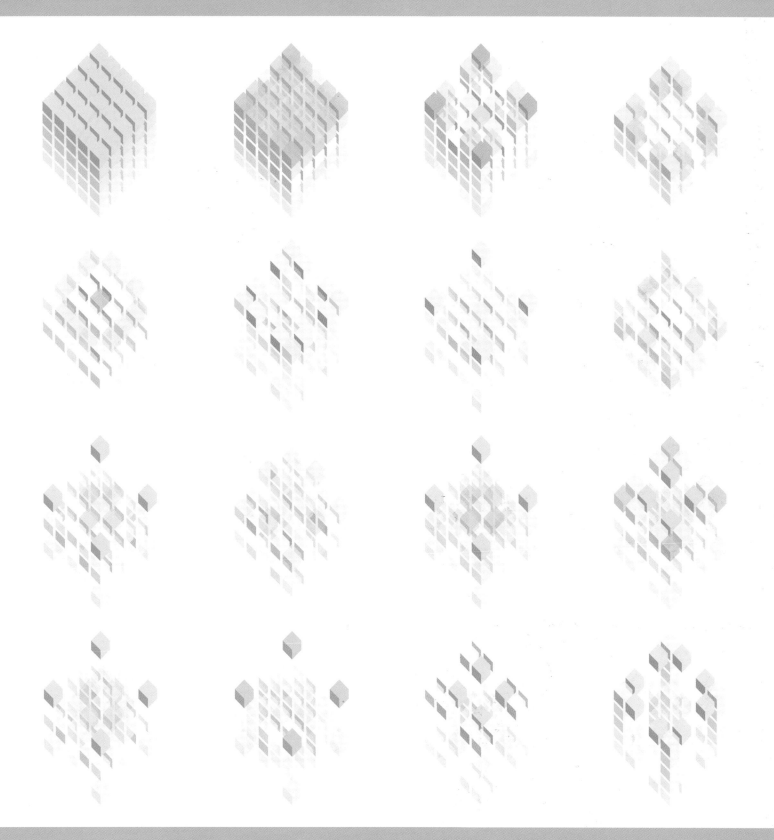

Title: Cubes   Description: Continually evolving screen saver, based on minimalist music and art
Medium: Web   Date: 2001–present   Design: Mark Harris

Title: Tumble   Description: Continually evolving screen saver, based on minimalist music and art   Medium: Web
Date: 2001-present   Design: Mark Harris

FLUID

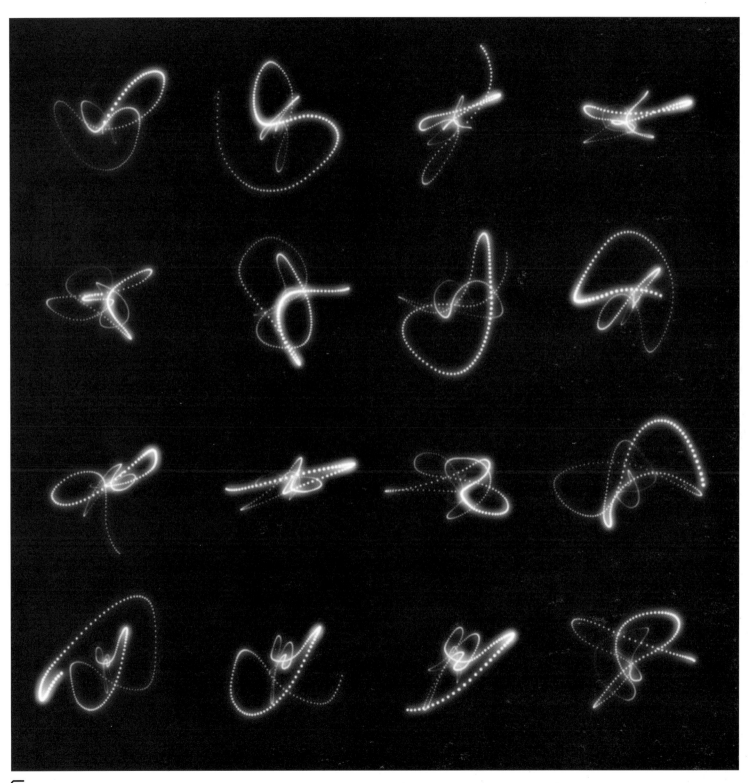

Title: Wiggle   Description: Continually evolving screen saver, based on minimalist music and art   Medium: Web
Date: 2001-present   Design: Mark Harris

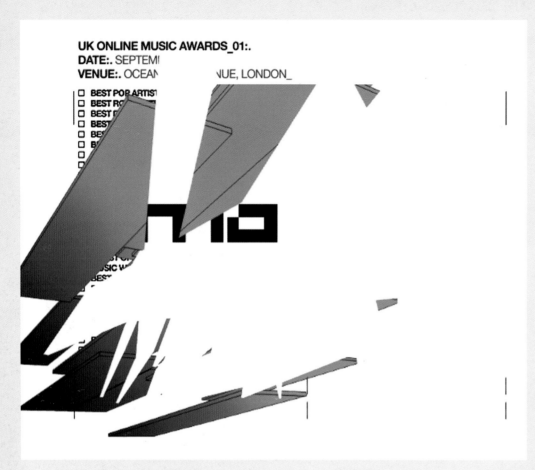

UK ONLINE MUSIC AWARDS_01:.
DATE:. SEPTEMI
VENUE:. OCEAN   NUE, LONDON_

☐ **BEST POP ARTIST**
☐ **BEST RO**
☐ **BEST**
☐ **BEST**
☐ **BE**
☐ **B**
☐
☐

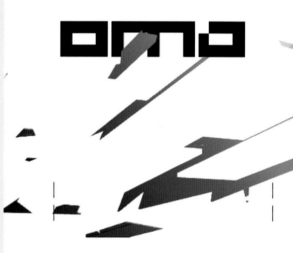

UK ONLINE MUSIC AWARDS_01:.

UK ONLINE MUSIC AWARDS_01:.
☐ **DESIGN PHASE_■**

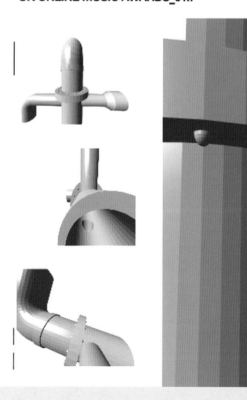

UK ONLINE MUSIC AWARDS_01:.

Title: UK Online Music Awards 01   Description: Video created for the Online Awards night   Medium: Video   Date: 2001

UK ONLINE MUSIC AWARDS_01:.
☐ DESIGN PHASE_■

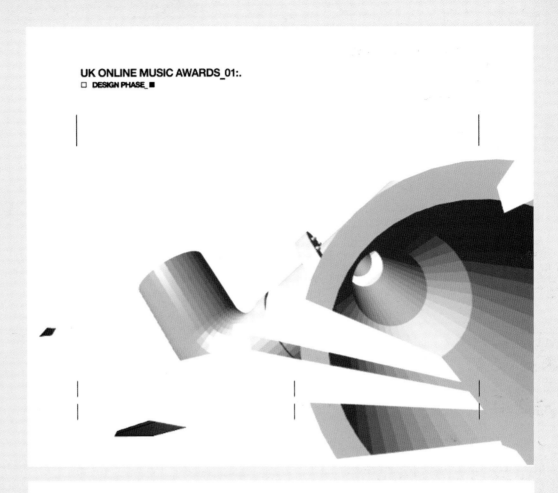

UK ONLINE MUSIC AWARDS_01:.
☐ OPTIONS_■

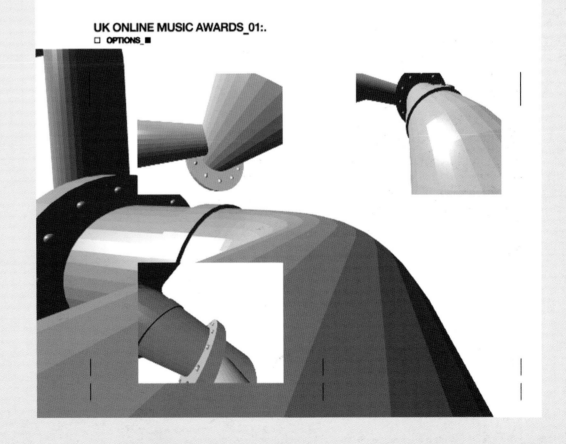

UK ONLINE MUSIC AWARDS_01:.

Title: UK Online Music Awards 01   Description: Video created for the Online Awards night   Medium: Video   Date: 2001

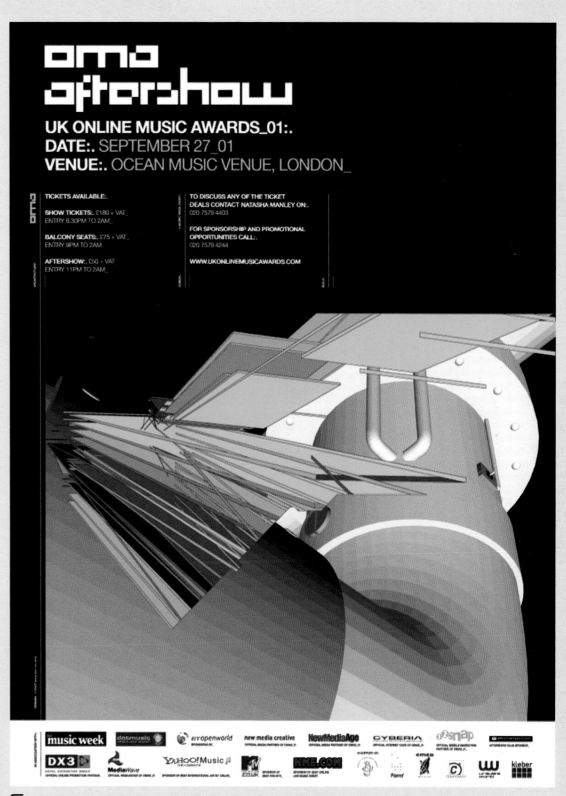

Title: UK Online Music Awards 01   Description: Advertising Campaign for OMA 01   Medium: Print   Date: 2001

Company **Foundation 33** Design Partners **Eatock / Solhaug**

Multi-Ply tables are constructed by laminating plywood strips that have been turned on edge. These components have been computer-cut following stringent patterns designed to systematically fit together, thus maximising the use of each standard 4 x 8 foot sheet of plywood by eliminating offcuts and waste. (See diagrams on opposite page.) This is a conceptually motivated design approach that minimises subjective decision-making.

The cutting and re-orienting of the plywood strips reveals the layered structure concealed within the sheet, forming a reconstructed surface of exposed edges. The finished tables are lighter than the original sheets of material. This difference in weight 'literally sawdust' is conceptually returned to each table as the numerical designation in the title.

All tables are meticulously constructed, reinforced with internal steel rods, and finished with multiple coats of clear lacquer that form precision-smooth surfaces of the highest possible standard.

Daniel Eatock: form through conceptual sequences / Sam Solhaug: dialectical form-making through process

All table designs ©2000 Daniel Eatock / Sam Solhaug / Copyright Protected by A©ID Anti Copying in Design

Thank you Martin Andersen / Andrew Blauvelt / Blu Dot / Timothy Evans / The Design Net / James Latham / Opus Magnum / Kathleen McLean / Orange Communications / Unit 26

Foundation 33 sponsored in part at Designers Block, 2000 by Tower Hamlets Cultural Industries Development Agency CIDA

Brochure design Daniel Eatock with input from Sam Solhaug / Printed by Xtraprint London

The Iterative and the Recursive: The Serial Logic of Multi-Ply
Andrew Blauvelt Design Director Walker Art Center

I have been searching for a term to describe the kind of systematic design that I have been interested in lately, which I find in three-dimensional form in the Multi-Ply series of furniture by Foundation 33. Precision, efficiency, rationality: these are the words that come to mind with the Multi-Ply series. There has always been something missing from the equation, as if the terms are borrowed wholesale from science or hold the vestiges of modernism. Such terminology misses, I believe, the conceptual nature of the work by being more descriptive of its technical execution. It is only with the occasion of the Multi-Ply series—the 10.2 Coffee Table, 16.8 Dining Table, and the 8.4 Low Table—that the conceptual logic reveals itself. The Multi-Ply series explicates the recursive nature of the process. The recursive structure is one in which some of the elements produce the rules that generate the structure itself. In this way the Multi-Ply series reveals the generative nature of the working method in which recurring elements (the material, the method of assembly, the numbering function of the titles) establish continuity yet yield variation. By contrast, iteration is repetition, which is the logic of modern industrial production. In their exhibition space at 100% Design [October 2000], Foundation 33 uses the material of repetition—mirrored glass. By fabricating only half of each table—their formation interrupted—and displaying it against a mirrored wall, the completion of the object is realised. However, the serial logic of Multi-Ply remains open and generative.

Title: Multi-Ply Tables   Description: Brochure for furniture designs in plywood, steel and lacquer   Medium: Print   Date: 2000   Designed with Sam Solhaug

Buy a Multi-Ply table...
Angus Hyland and a guy from
Texas have, and Peter Saville
said he would...

Daniel Eatock / Sam Solhaug
www.foundation33.com

⤷ Title: Multi-ply Tables   Description: Advertisement for furniture design in DotDotDot magazine
(graphic design and visual culture)   Medium: Print   Date: 2000   Designed with Sam Solhaug

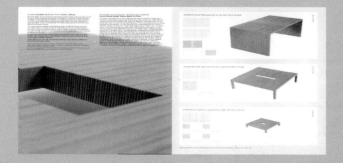

Title: UK Hip-Hop   Description: Promotional CD designed for cover of a hip-hop magazine   Medium: CD-ROM   Date: 2001

JOSH FULLER

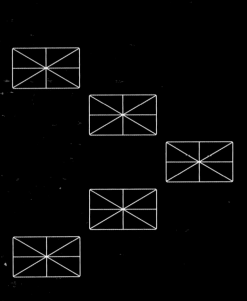

JAMES GOGGIN

Title: Vapour Trail T-shirt   Description: White flocked print on sky-blue cotton for the collection All Weather   Medium: Textile print   Date: 2001

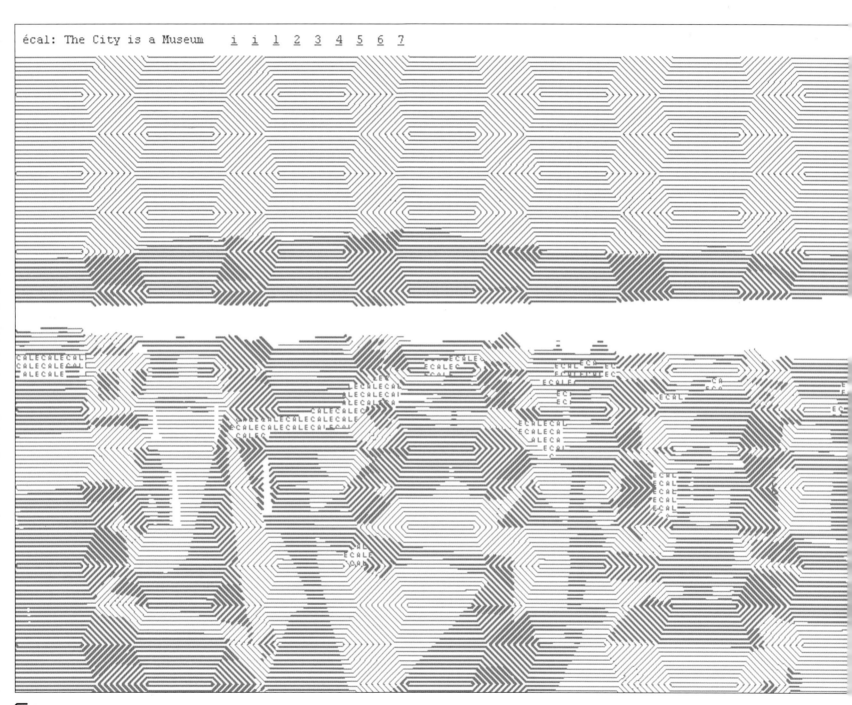

écal: The City is a Museum   i i 1 2 3 4 5 6 7

⌐ Title: The City is a Museum   Description: A web workshop project with Ecole Cantonale d'Art de Lausanne, Switzerland   Medium: Web   Date: 2001

JAMES GOGGIN

Title: Adidas 2001 Description: Adidas advertisement shown in The Face magazine Medium: Print Date: 2001

adidas 2001 © robert green

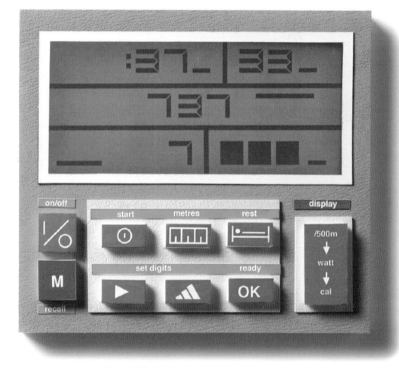

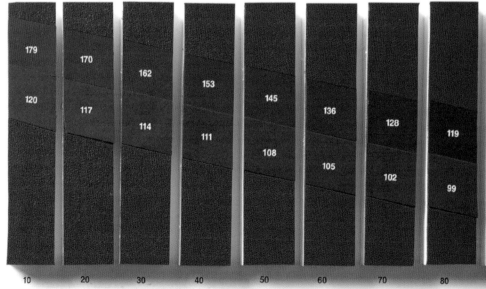

Title: CCTV   Description: Oversize stickers for window graphic at the Thirst bar, Oxford   Medium: Print   Date: 2002
Illustration: Susumu Mukai   Art Direction, Design and Digital Colouring: Robert Green

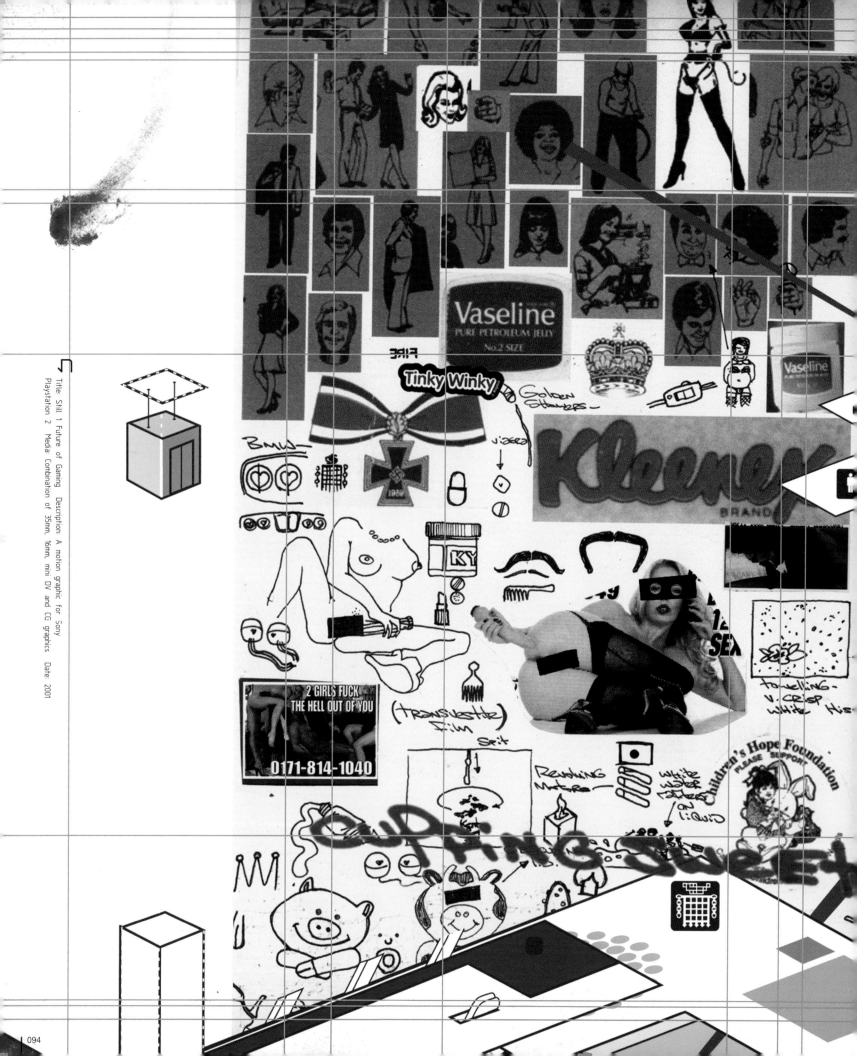

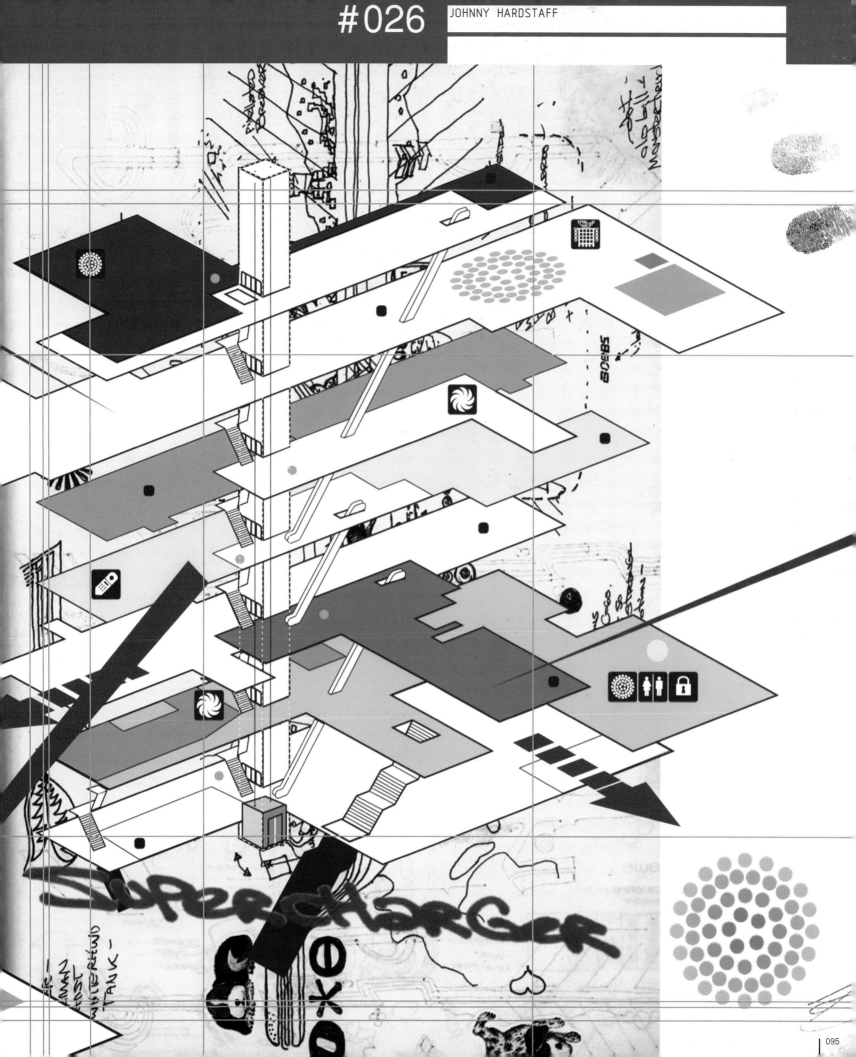

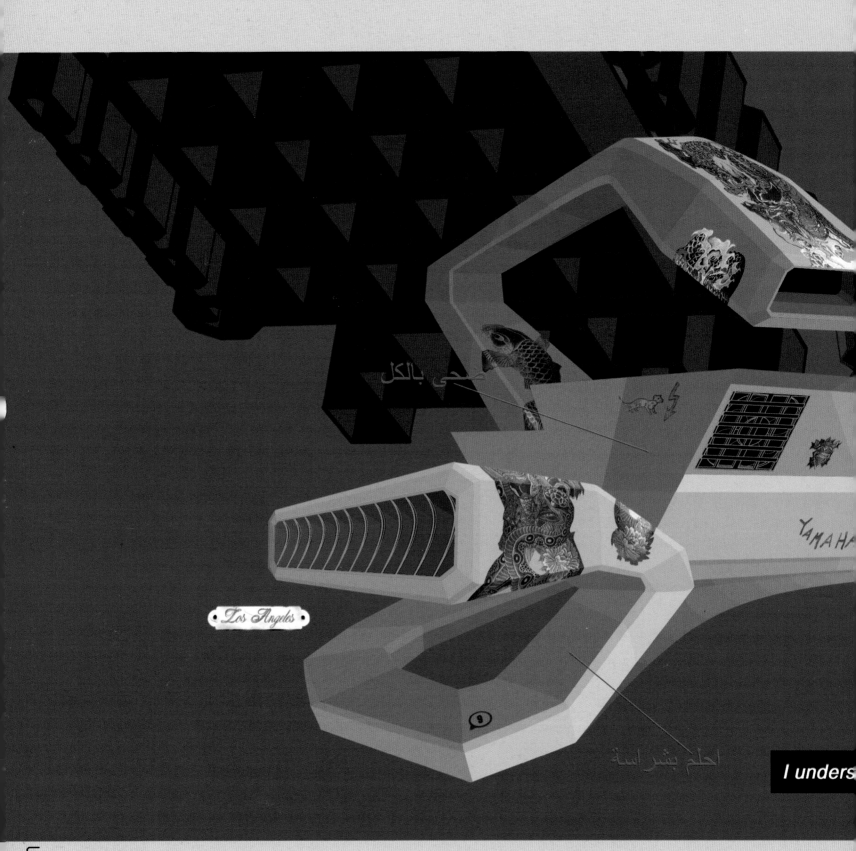

ضحى بالكل

Los Angeles

YAMAHA

⑨

احلم بشر اسنة

I unders

Title: Still 2 Future Of Gaming   Description: A motion graphic for Sony Playstation 2
Media: Combination of 35mm, 16mm, mini DV and CG graphics   Date: 2001

JOHNNY HARDSTAFF

الخوف هو الظلام الذي نحمله في رأسنا

MARION

دمك قلعتي

يقوم برد فعل ضاري

Playstation 2.

Post-it note. Sizes shown, 3x4" 3x3" 1.5x2" 2x3" . Overleaf 3x5"

The YSCN is supported by the British Association and Think-Lab

Title: Young Science Communicators' Network   Description: A reuseable information card   Medium: Print   Date: 2001

Young Science Communicators' Network

3

The Young Science Communicators' Network is a group of science communicators in the early stages of their careers who meet to exchange information, ideas and experiences, helping to make science communication a more professional field.

The group networks both electronically and face to face, through an internet based discussion list and a programme of events and activities throughout the year, ranging from training events to informal get-togethers.

The network is always keen for new ideas and members, so if you work in, or study science communication and are under 35, you can join the network by sending a blank e-mail to us at yscn-subscribe@topica.com

Contact   www.yscn.org.uk   info@yscn.org.uk

Title: U2: Stuck In A Moment You Can't Get Out Of   Description: Packaging for U2 CD (Special French Edition)   Medium: Print   Date: 2001

BLOCK
16 FIND AN
OASIS
FEATURING JHELISA

BLOCK
16 CAN'T
STOP
WITH ROBERT OWENS

BLOCK
16 MORNING
SUN

BLOCK
16 MORNING
SUN
FEATURING JON LUCIEN

↳ Title: Block 16   Description: Cover designs for a series of 12" album and single sleeves   Medium: Print
Date: 2001   Illustration: Danny Boons   Designed with Danny Boyle

Röyksopp
Eple

⤷ Title: Röyksopp: Eple   Description: Sleeve for 12" single   Medium: Print   Date: 2001   Photography: Sølve Sundsbø

MASSIVE ATTACK: ELEVEN PROMOS/DVD

7243 492631 9 2

7 24349 26319 2

UK-VDVD06 F: PM902 LC03098 Printed in the E.U.

I2

Title: Massive Attack: Eleven Promos DVD   Description: DVD packaging   Medium: Print   Date: 2001   Designed with Robert Del Naja

Skrean©

A Family of six typefaces, set in three styles with three italics
Designer: Nick Hayes
Over 180 Characters

Skrean Regular

AaBbCCDdEEFFGgHhIiJJKKLlMMNnOOPPQgRrSSTtUUUUWWXXYYZZ1234567890

Skrean Regular Italic

AaBbCCDdEEFFGgHhIiJJKKLlMMNnOOPPQgRrSSTtUUUUWWXXYYZZ

Skrean Regular Negative

AaBbCCDdEEFFGgHhIiJJKKLlMMNnOOPPQgRrSSTtUUUUWWXXYYZZ

Skrean Regular

AaBbCCDdEEFFGgHhIiJJKKLlMMNnOOPPQgRrSSTtUUUUWWXXYYZZ1234567890

Skrean Regular Italic

AaBbCCDdEEFFGgHhIiJJKKLlMMNnOOPPQgRrSSTtUUUUWWXXYYZZ

Skrean Regular Negative

AaBbCCDdEEFFGgHhIiJJKKLlMMNnOOPPQgRrSSTtUUUUWWXXYYZZ

>>IDENTIKAL_CORP//0034296S__
SYSTEMS_MODIFIED@_2002
***Syntax_Error@_CODEWARE?S
RE-BOOT::::::::

SKREAN>>FONt

SKREAN_FONt_WILL_MAKE_YOUR_WORK_LOOK_UNIQUE_&_FRESH_USE_IT_to_ADD_Xtra_DETAIL_*2130

Title: Skrean   Description: A family of six typefaces from The Identikal Foundry 4   Medium: Print   Date: 2001

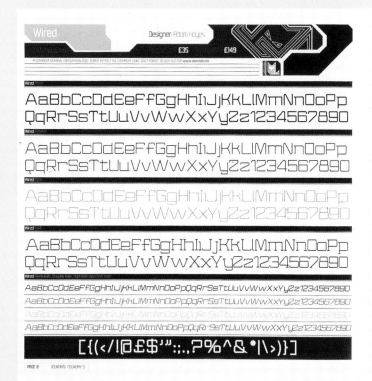

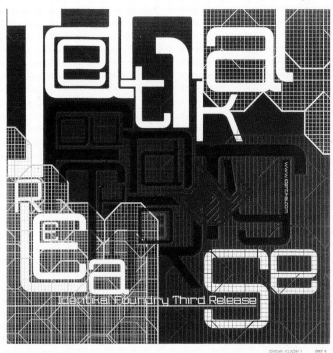

Title: Wired   Description: New 200-character fonts from The Identikal Foundry 3   Medium: Print   Date: 2001

Title: Trak   Description: New 200-character typefaces from The Identikal Foundry 3   Medium: Print   Date: 2001

ABCDEFGHIJ
KLMNOPQRS
TUVWXYZ

abcdefghijklmn
opqrtuvwxyz

1234567890

Title: Wired Black font   Date: 2001

ABCDEFGHIJ
KLMNOPQRS
TUVWXYZ
abcdefghijklmn
opqrtuvwxyz
1234567890

Title: Trak Regular font   Date: 2001

ABCDEFGHIJ
KLMNOPQRS
TUVWXYZ
abcdefghijklmn
opqrtuvwxyz
1234567890

Title: Trak Black font   Date: 2001

ABCDEFGHIJ
KLMNOPQRS
TUVWXYZ
abcdefghijklmn
opqrtuuwxyz
1234567890

graphic
britain

GB

ABCDEFGHIJ
KLMNOPQRS
TUVWXYZ
abcdefghijklmn
opqrtuuwxyz
1234567890

ABCDEFGHIJ
KLMNOPQRS
TUVWXYZ
abcdefghijklmn
opqrtuuwxyz
1234567890

↳ Title: Skrean Light font   Date: 2001   (above)
Title: Skrean Regular font   Date: 2001   (below)

↳ Title: Skrean Light Negative font   Date: 2001   (above)
Title: Skrean Regular Negative font   Date: 2001   (below)

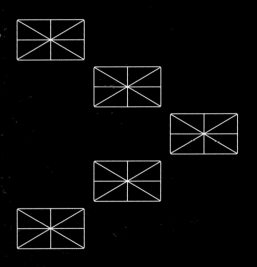

Title: Moving Surnames Description: Detail of shadow sculpture wall piece at Cayenne restaurant, Belfast Medium: Digitally milled Corrian Date: 2001 Design: Peter Anderson

Title: Cayenne Matchbox   Description: Cover design for matchbox listing all the names of the restaurant staff   Medium: Print   Date: 2001
Design: Peter Anderson

Title: Cayenne Coasters   Description: Paper coasters designed with lines from a food limerick   Medium: Print   Date: 2001   Design: Peter Anderson

Title: Cayenne Menu   Description: Menu showing names from the Northern
Ireland phone book, visually linked to the shadow sculpture Moving Surnames
Medium: Print   Date: 2001   Design: Peter Anderson

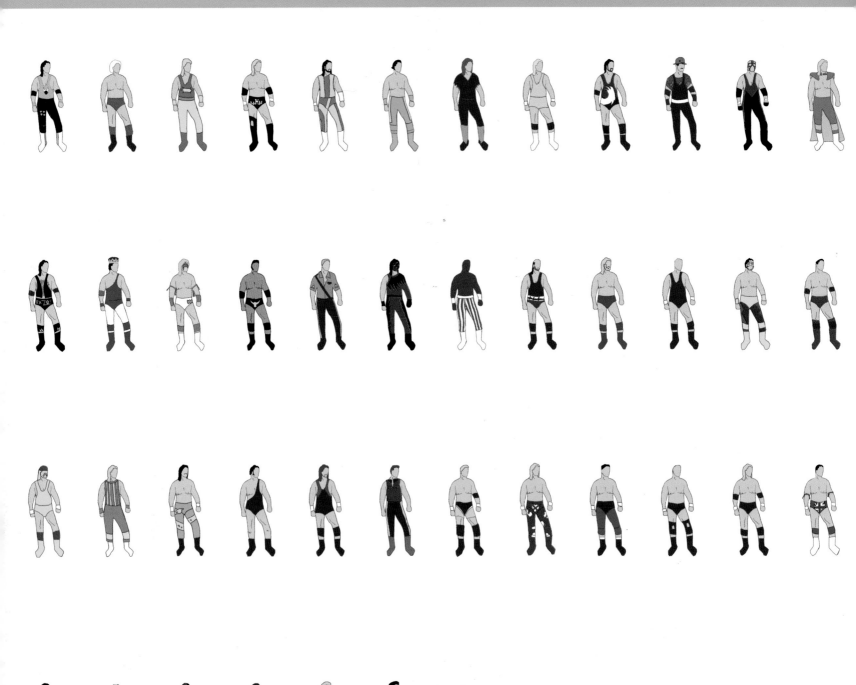

Title: Gimics   Description: A personal poster design shown in exhibition   Medium: Print   Date: 2001

LEE JEPSON

Title: Mullet XI Description: Promotional poster shown in Nottingham during the European Football Championships Medium: Print Date: 2001

1.goalkeeper

2.right back

4.centre back

5.centre back

3.left back

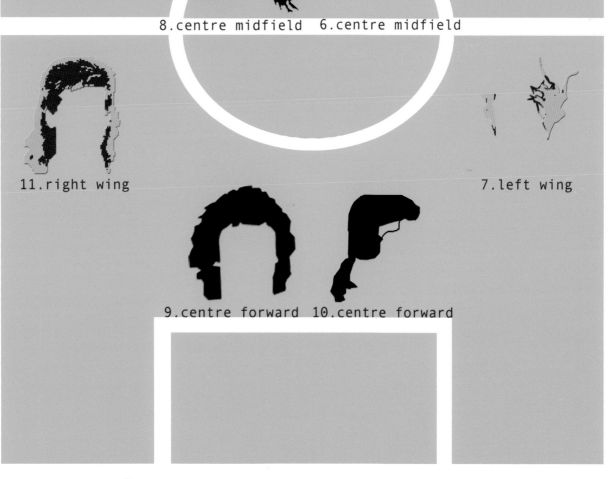

8.centre midfield   6.centre midfield

11.right wing

7.left wing

9.centre forward   10.centre forward

TRUTH ABOUT SMOKING

IMPOTENT YELLOW SKIN

annoying cough **ANEREXIC** BANKRUPT

BAD BREATH BLADDER PROBLEMS

Title: Tabs   Description: Series of posters for exhibition   Medium: Print   Date: 2001

LEE JEPSON

TRUTH ABOUT SMOKING

MANS BEST FRIEND

PASSIVE SMOKING CAN CAUSE CANCER IN PETS
ESPECIALLY SHORT NOSED DOGS

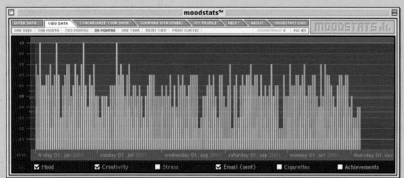

Title: Moodstats   Description: "Emotional software" application used to monitor moods and habits   Medium: Web   Date: 2001-2002

Title: Impress   Description: Cover illustration for Impress magazine   Medium: Print   Date: 2002

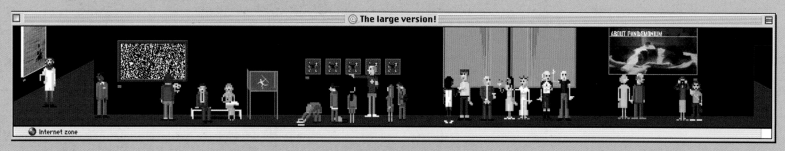

Title: Pandaemonium   Description: Audio-visual installation exhibited in Pandaemonium biennial at The Lux, London   Media: Mixed media   Date: 2001

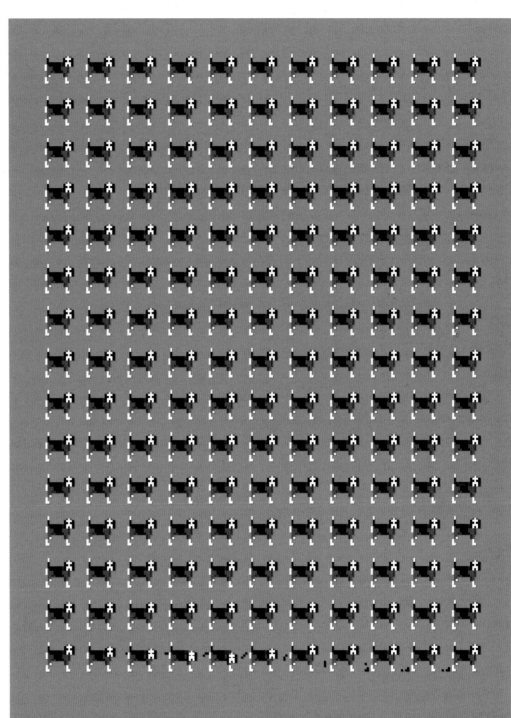

project save the LPC

LITTLE PIXEL CREATURES HAVE FEELINGS TOO. HELP THEM HELP THEMSELVES
HUMAN RIGHTS IN 2001

Title: Barney Poster   Description: Poster featuring the fictional house pet Barney The Beagle, created for online design store Threadless   Medium: Web and print   Date: 2002

VINTAGEX GROSS

PHOTOGRAPHY_PIERS NORTH | STYLIST_LAIA FARRAN | MODEL_NODE CUNNINGHAM @ NEW STENCH STUDIOS

Cutler & Gross Vintage is the new shop dedicated to vintage eyewear. For Mr Gross - the brainchild behind this operation... "the store is for fashion people to sell fashion, not for collectors". In conjuction with Marie Wilkinson, this unique shop has opened to sell sunglasses and frames dating from the late 1950s through to the 1990s. Tony Gross has collected glasses all his life. One can see his true passion when talking about eyewear; he is animated and reaches out for examples as he talks about different anecdotes and trends. Above all he is fun and full of charm. When I ask him to pick out his favourite pair, he struggles and finally opts for a pair kept under a big glass case table. It is the biggest pair of sunglasses I have ever seen, and they have a french flag across the front of them (opposite page). "I got this off a guy who had committed suicide and left all his belongings to be sold on. It was in Paris in a flea market, I thought I had seen everything until I saw them!" Another favourite of Tony's was the 1972 Cortina Olympics official sunglasses. The glasses range between £100/£200 a pair, some are more expensive, for example the hand-crafted Courèges which are £300. The store has a fantastic range from Pierre Cardin's early work, Pucci, and Christian Dior, including a limited edition of Brigitte Bardot styles. Why this passion for sunglasses? It turns out Tony loves the glamour behind the original sunglasses - junkies. "...to wear sunglasses when they were first designed you had to be a spy or a movie star, it was glamorous and I love it!" - Tony laughs mischievously. Old style and glamour meet in an ultra modern environment, resulting in an Aladdin's cave of glasses from the ridiculous to the sublime. A cutting-edge store, by the architects - Softroom, where classics style meets the future.
The Cutler & Gross Vintage shop is located at 7 Knightsbridge Green, London SW1

Title: Vintage Gross   Description: Photographic spread from Lab02 magazine   Medium: Print   Date: 2001   Photographer: Piers North

---

SINCLAIR SPECTRUM

TEXT BARBARELLA
PHOTOGRAPHER DAVE FOSTER
COOPERATION WAYNE MAXTED

RETRO SPECTRUM

The early 1980's were great times. There were great television shows like Scooby Doo and The Cosby Show, games like the Rubik's cube, Atari, and Coleco. It was also the age of great pop music like Madonna, Duran Duran, Depeche Mode, Boy George, Cyndi Lauper, Bananarama and Eurythmics; the list is endless. Yep, there were great times. With all that you probably think that nothing could have been much better. Well, you'd be surprised that out of all the great things about the earlier 1980's (and late 1980's too), a small chunk of plastic, chips and wire were actually one of the greatest things the 1980's were all about. Its name was the Sinclair Spectrum, a compact home computer that was huge in its day, broke barriers and set standards in home computing to be admired today. In 1980 Clive Sinclair did what everyone said was impossible. With the Sinclair ZX80 he was the first man to make a computer that broke the psychological barrel of £100, finally making computing affordable for everyone who wanted to give it a go. If you were brave you could buy it in kit form for £79.95 and solder it together, or you could save yourself £20 worth of heartache and get it ready-built for £99.95. The machine had a flat membrane keypad, measured 9" x 7", was plugged to a TV and cassette drive to display and store programs and used the now famous single keyword entry method for its Sinclair Basic programming language. The ZX80 - the world's smallest and cheapest computer - was launched at an exhibition in Wembley at the end of January 1980. It was tiny, really tiny, and weighed almost as much as a baguette. One of the biggest savings in order to keep the price low was the use of a domestic television

set as a screen and a cassette player as a program and data store. Whoever owned one probably remembers the amount of time that had to be spent setting the correct volume in the cassette recorder, synthonizing the TV channel, and trying to load games and programs getting it right (which rarely happened the first time). The ZX80 was very much aimed at the person in the street wanting to know something about programming computers. Sinclair was convinced that people could be persuaded to buy the ZX80 but how to persuade them was the problem. The image of the computer at that time was still somewhat Big Brother: clinical, air-conditioned surroundings, huge cabinets with reels of magnetic tape whirring to and fro. How would people relate such a frightening piece of equipment to the ZX80? Why would they want to buy it for the home? Why would they want to buy it at all? No one need have worried. The ZX80 was an immediate success; ten orders were placed at the exhibition in the first five minutes and thousands were sold afterwards. Although primitive compared even to the ZX81 and the Spectrum, it laid the pattern for virtually every Sinclair machine to come. It was the smallest and cheapest computer in the world and was one of the first aimed at the home user, as opposed to the hobbyist. Nonetheless, it marked a key point in the development of Sinclair and the British computer market. The second leap was the ZX81, launched in March 1981. It had a membrane keyboard like the ZX80 but with a more complex version of Sinclair Basic and cost £69.95. Like the earlier machine, the ZX81 was available both as a kit, at £49.95, and in a fully manufactured form at £69.95. Although

eclipsed by the ZX Spectrum in the memories of both commentators and consumers, the ZX81 microcomputer is undoubtedly the most important product to emerge from the Sinclair stable. Technologically, the ZX81 was something really quite special. It was a real computer, you could do calculations, it was programmable, you could do lots of things with it - it was in every way a real computer at a very low price. With the success of the ZX81, Sinclair found himself in the role of evuncular guru for an entire generation of microcomputing enthusiasts. The Spectrum, launched in April 1982, was the biggest coup for Sir Clive. For the first time, here was a powerful computer with enough Ram for serious applications and the ability to produce colour graphics, all for under £200. At last, Sinclair Research was notionally able to compete with the BBC Micro and other personal computers; the figures in the table published in the ZX Spectrum leaflet were impressive. The ZX81 had been competing against the Acorn Atom; it could never have stood up against the BBC model A, the current Acorn competitor when the Spectrum came

out. The Spectrum had a more versatile Sinclair Basic than the previous two machines; an improved keyboard replaced the unpopular - though cheap - touch-sensitive keyboard; it was able to generate and display 49,152 pixels in 8 colours. The low cost of the Spectrum meant that parents were prepared to buy them to give their children 'a good start in life'. What sort of computer you had become an important factor in playground status. The place of the computer in the home was reinforced by the meagre provision in schools, where there was often only one machine between 30 pupils and thus insufficient opportunity for everyone to practice. What better solution than a computer at home? The membrane keyboard of the ZX81 was a great success and Sinclair has had to cope with numerous pirate copies since its inception but, as with everything, it had its disadvantages. Its main disadvantage was its inability to register touch. To ensure you had a response it was necessary to look at the screen - there was no reassuring click when you touched each key. For the Spectrum, award-winning industrial designer Rick Dickinson had

returned to a raised keyboard but again he produced a first by making it from rubber. The keyboard comprised a one-piece grey rubber moulding mounted over a pressure-sensitive membrane. The keys poked up through holes in a black metal plate and the feel was more that of a calculator than a typewriter. Most keytops have three symbols on them and, in addition, most of them have another two associated inscriptions printed on the metal surround. A sort of cross between Scrabble, The Periodic Table and cross-puzzles. Sounds complicated. It just took a while to get used to. Who doesn't miss those hieroglyphic keyboards today, and the soft, velveted and cushioned touch they had? So there it goes. Mission impossible. A brief peek into what computing in the 80's was all about. Unfortunately, Sir Clive Sinclair's descent was nearly as swift as his rise. Unable to cope with the massive market request (in Easter Sinclair Research were selling an incredible 12,000 Spectrums a week), and in a desperate hurry to beat the launch of Apple's Macintosh micro, Sinclair's pattern of late deliveries and unreliability had begun to emerge, anticipating a

fatal and inevitable crash. In October 1984 Sinclair Research unwittingly signed its own death warrant. Distributors had widely overstocked with the Spectrum Plus (Spectrum's successor) at Christmas and when the market nose-dived in January, Sinclair Research became desperate for money; just when nobody wanted to re-order. Sinclair looked for partners to help him weather the storm, with no success, and less than 8 weeks later, at a hastily called press conference, a subdued Sir Clive handed over all marketing, production and distribution rights to his computer products arch rival Alan Sugar at Amstrad. The whole business he had built up over seven years turned over lock stock and barrel for a mere £5 million.
The name of Sinclair computers now rests in peace in the mausoleum of retro computers, where tons of fans join today to persevere, hunt, and rescue what was to be one of the biggest - and shortest - achievements in the history of home computing. Long live Sinclair!

SINCLAIR ZX81 AND ZX80

Title: Retro Spectrum   Description: Article in Lab02 magazine   Medium: Print   Date: 2001

PORTFOLIO: TNOP /ti-nop/ n. is a senior designer at Segura-inc., a design firm in Chicago. He's origially from Thailand. He works and lives in the US since 1996. His real name is Teeranop Wangsillapakun, but he shortened it to TNOP for obvious reasons... let the images speak for themselves. www.tnop.com

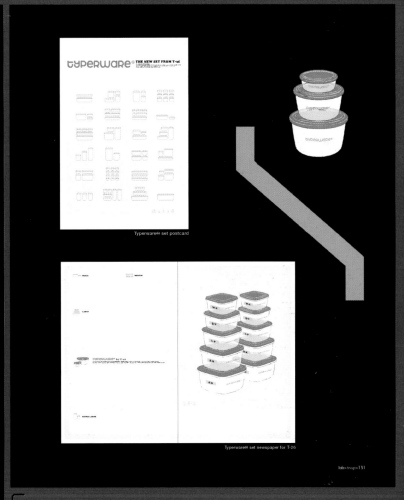

Typerware® set postcard

Typerware® set newspaper for T-26

Detail of a Typerware® set newspaper designed for T-26 (digital type foundry)

Title: TNOP   Description: Design feature in Lab02 magazine   Medium: Print   Date: 2001

>micro02

TEXTS: ALEX TOVEY, LAIA FARRAN, TEVI DE LA TORRE, PHOEBE JASIAK

▼
01

SOFTWEAR>

SOFT PHONE > Technology and style have long been divorced but Lab are glad to announce a happy reunion with the introduction of the Soft Phone. Employing cutting edge technology, the Soft Phone can change from a mobile phone handset to a 007 style wrist phone. The soft Elektex body is a well styled piece of equipment with a removable phone module. In Layman's terms, you can remove the technology from the body and introduce it to other modules for different usage. No more sore thumbs from trawling through names in your phone book, the Soft Phone uses a simple stroking action when searching for numbers, and with and ICD interface in place of a number pad, even those boys from NASA will be jealous of your wrist action. www.ideo.com / www.elektex.com

lab>micro>08

▶
02

WORN-IN>

HOME LAUNDRY > Levi's red tab home laundry range is a modern and entirely original interpretation of classic vintage cuts. In keeping with current 80's trends, worn-in denim wear transpires in new black and blue glossy contrast. Corduroy, leather and denim complete this capsule range for men and women with energy and style. Trailer trash eat your heart out! Available from Levi's stores worldwide. www.levis.com

lab>micro>09

Title Micro 02   Description Part of the Micro bulletin section in
Lab02 magazine   Medium Print   Date 2001

PINK HAT WITH NET BY **KATHERINE HAMNETT** + TOP BY **TOPSHOP** + LOOP COLOURED DIAMANTÉ BELT BY **BUTLER & WILSON** + KNICKERS BY **TOBY PIMLICO** + DIAMANTÉ SHOES BY **JIMMY CHOO**

HELLO KITTY T-SHIRT BY SANRIO @ SELFRIDGES + KNICKERS BY HANDER KNITTING @ TOPSHOP + ARM BAND BY STONE ISLAND + WHITE LEGWARMERS BY TOPSHOP + GREY SHOES BY LK BENNETT + SILVER CHARM BRACELET BY LYNX

Title: Physical Description: Fashion spread in Lab02 magazine
Medium: Print Date: 2001 Photographer: Andrew Hobbs

Title: Less Rain Portfolio   Description: Part of online portfolio from ‹lessrain.co.uk›   Medium: Web   Date: 2001

LOCATION DATE   TEMPERATURE HUMIDITY WIND   OUTLOOK

PORTFOLIO   PROJECT

PROJECTS **98 99 00** 01 **BROCHURE**

SCREENSHOTS

Title: Andrew Cross Portfolio   Description: An online portfolio and book of photographs   Media: Web and print   Date: 2001

Andrew Cross has been working as a photographer since 1999 and his photographs have appeared in various publications including Artforum, Blueprint, Themepark, and the Archibitects' Journal. Clients include Saab, Swindon Borough Council, Hawkins Brown Architects, V&A Publications, Minetta Brook New York and August Media/Berkhauser. He is currently undertaking a landscape photography commission through the University of Sunderland and is preparing a book of his American railroad photographs. Before becoming a photographer he established the reputation as an exhibitions curator. Work with which he is still involved. Recent curatorial projects include Asia City (Photographers Gallery, London 1998) School Reunion (Anthony Wilkinson Gallery London 1999) and Real Places? (Westfälischer Kunstverein, Münster 2000). He also organised the conference Transport, Technology and Sense of Place at London's Stansted Airport (1999). ANDREW@ANDREWCROSS.CO.UK   0044 20 888 8888

This site shows a selection of photographs taken from current and recent projects. All images shown on this Website are the copyright of Andrew Cross and must not be reproduced without prior permission. All images originate as C-type prints and are available in a range of sizes.

BACK TO LESSRAIN   ANDREW CROSS INFO PHOTOGRAPHY

Title: Less Rain   Description: Online portfolio from <www.lessrain.de>   Medium: Web   Date: 2001   Photographers: Andrew Cross, Sonja Mueller and Ronald Dick

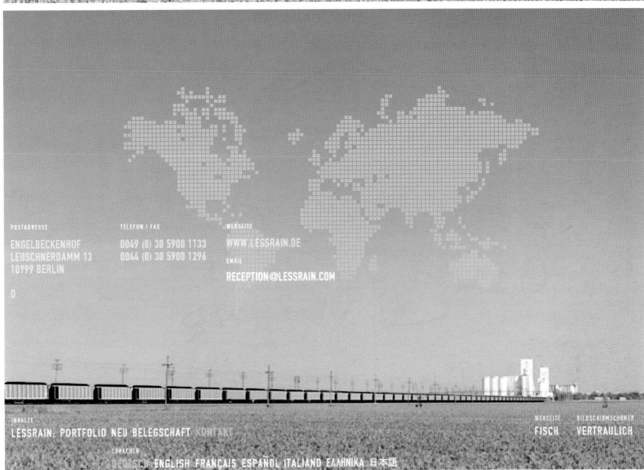

POSTADRESSE   TELEFON / FAX   WEBSEITE
ENGELBECKENHOF   0049 (0) 30 5900 1133   WWW.LESSRAIN.DE
LEUSCHNERDAMM 13   0044 (0) 30 5900 1296   EMAIL
10999 BERLIN   RECEPTION@LESSRAIN.COM
D

INHALTE
LESSRAIN. PORTFOLIO NEU BELEGSCHAFT KONTAKT   WEBSEITE BILDSCHIRMSCHONER
                                                              FISCH   VERTRAULICH
SPRACHEN
DEUTSCH ENGLISH FRANÇAIS ESPAÑOL ITALIANO ΕΛΛΗΝΙΚΑ 日本語

DONE

JR COMMENTS:

DRAW

JR E-MAIL: your_mail@your_domain

UPLOAD DISCARD

NGE LOCATION   SOUND ON   DISCONNECT

Title: Eyes Only   Description: CD-ROM and internet art project ‹www.lessrain.com/eyesonly› based on the observation of UFOs   Medium: CD-ROM and web   Date: 2001

ARFAK   ON-LINE   MARCH 23 2001   12 38

ANGE LOCATION   SOUND ON   DISCONNECT

CONTENTS
LESSRAIN: PORTFOLIO NEW TEAM JOBS CONTACT
WEBSITE   SCREENSAVER
FISH   EYES ONLY

Title: Eyes Only   Description: Website screen saver taken from the Eyes Only art project   Medium: CD-ROM and web   Date: 2001

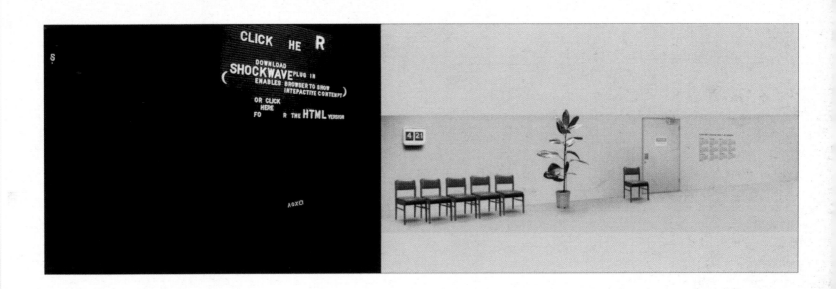

PROJECT
sony playstation uk

LOCATION
www.uk.playstation.com

DATE
march - august 2000

Title: Sony Playstation UK   Description: Detail of Playstation 2 web page from print version of Less Rain Portfolio entitled 10mm   Media: Print and web   Date: 2000

Title: Less Rain Homepage   Description: Homepage for Less Rain website ‹www.lessrain.co.uk›   Medium: Web   Date: 2001-present

CONTENTS

LESSRAIN: PORTFOLIO NEW TEAM JOBS CONTACT

LANGUAGES

WEBSITE   SCREENSAVER

FISH   **EYES ONLY**

Title: Door Panel   Description: Part of the Smart Car exhibition at the Frankfurt Motor Show   Media: Marker pen on door panel
Date: 2001   Photographer: Jonathan Oppong-Wiafe

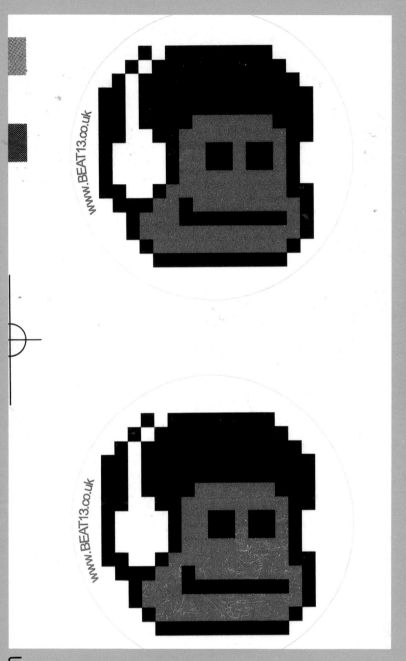

Title: Beat13/Graphic Equalizers   Description: Stickers for ‹www.beat13.co.uk›   Media: Print and web
Date: 2001   Designed with Matt Watkins, Al Murphy and Tim Watkins

CREDITS 01

Title: V's   Description: A personal project for exhibition   Media: Marker pen on plywood   Date: 2001   Photographer: Jonathan Oppong-Wiafe

Title: Peeps-Fight   Description: A personal project for exhibition   Media: Marker pen on plywood   Date: 2001   Photographer: Matt Watkins

LUCY MCLAUCHLAN

Title: Beat13/Graphic Equalizers   Description: Illustration for Beat 13 postcard   Media: Print and web
Date: 2001   Designed with Matt Watkins, Al Murphy and Tim Watkins

Badly Drawn Boy / featuring **Doves**

in ROADMOVIE
ROADMOVIE
ROADMOVIE
ROADMOVIE
ROADMOVIE
ROADMOVIE

10/8/98

 TWISTED NERVE

written by Damon Gough
performed live with Doves
at Frank Bough Sound II
recorded & mixed by
Jez Williams/Damon Gough

XL RECORDINGS.

45rpm

TNXL001r.

 Title: Road Movie   Description: Sleeve and record design for the Badly Drawn Boy single Featuring Doves   Media: Photography and print   Date: 1998

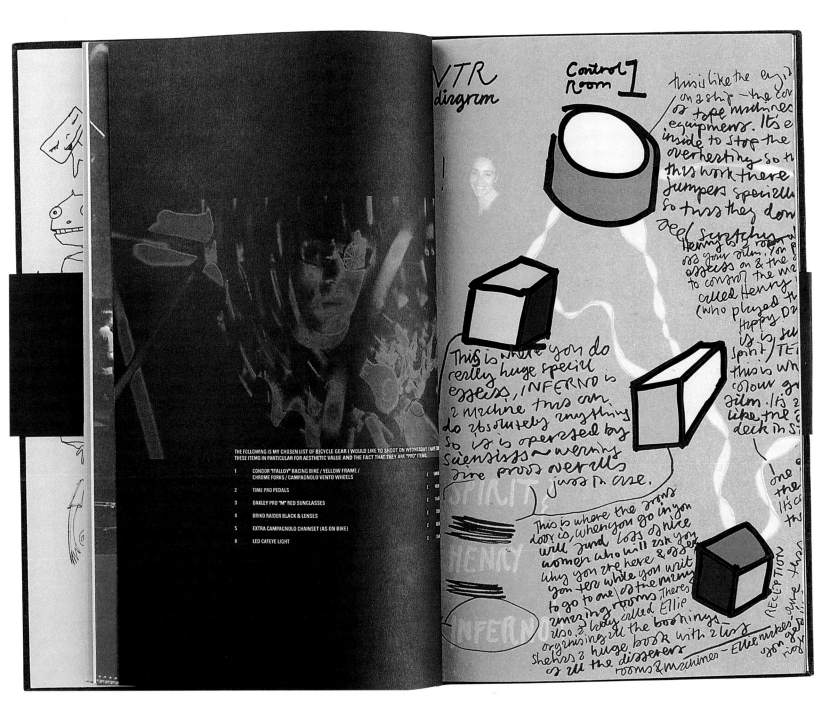

Title: VTR Diagram: Control Room 1   Description: Book and page design for Hammer and Tongs book   Medium: Print   Date: 1999

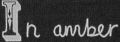**In** amber
produced by Tony Lash
engineered by Matthew Ollivier
recorded at Jacobs Studios
mixed by Dave Eringa at
Brittania Row.

Can't say no
produced by Tony Lash
engineered by Matthew Ollivier
recorded at Jacobs Studios
mixed by Tony Lash.

The feelings
produced by Tony Lash
engineered by Matthew Ollivier
recorded at Jacobs Studios
mixed by Pat Collier
at Gravity Shack.

God willing
produced by Lowgold
engineered by Pat Collier
& recorded at Gravity Shack
mixed by Pat Collier
at Gravity Shack.

Ⓟ&Ⓒ 2000 NUDE RECORDS LTD.
NUDE RECORDS, 5 WARREN MEWS, LONDON W1P 5DJ
http://www.nuderecords.com
DISTRIBUTED BY JMV/PINNACLE
A NUDE RECORD.

Title: Lowgold: The 108 EP   Description: Record sleeve design for the band Lowgold   Medium: Print   Date: 2000

Title: Let's Get Super-Charged!   Description: Light sculpture for exhibition based on a group of characters called Roods created by Mysteriousal   Medium: Neon light   Date: 2001

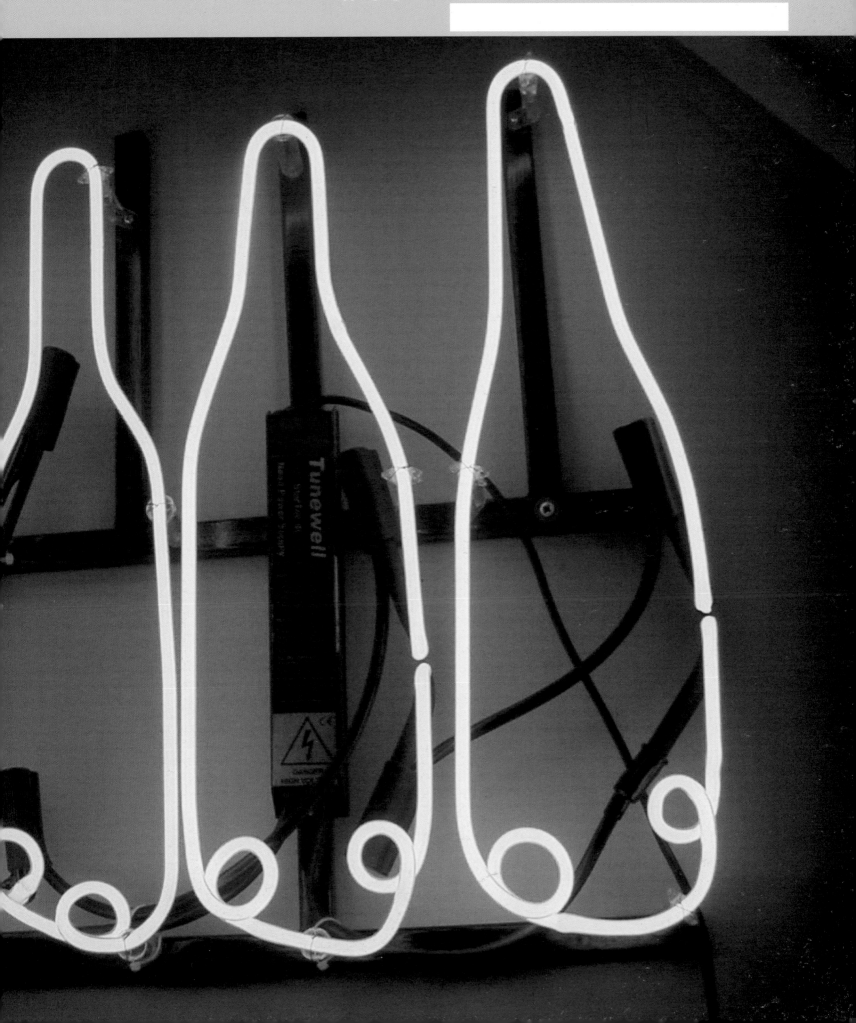

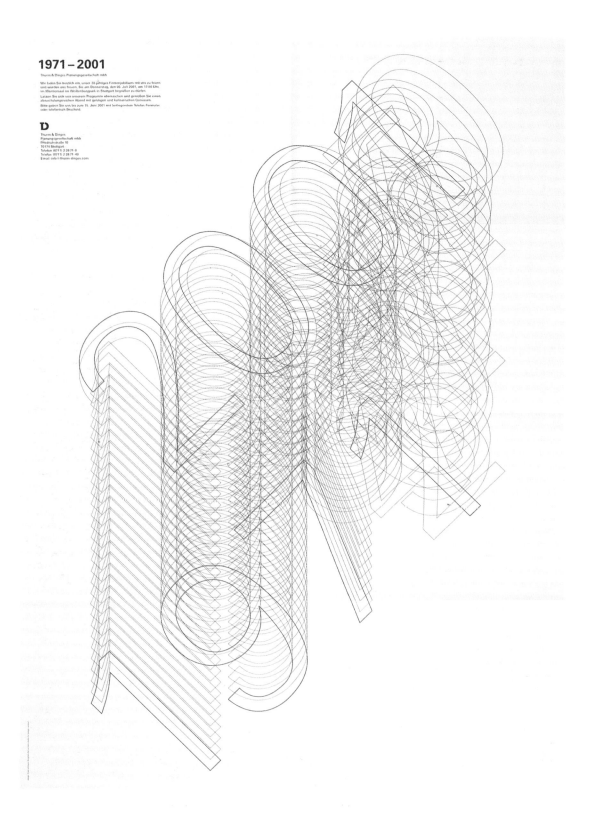

1971 – 2001

Thurm & Dinges Planungsgesellschaft mbh

Wir laden Sie herzlich ein, unser 30-jähriges Firmenjubiläum mit uns zu feiern
und würden uns freuen, Sie am Donnerstag, dem 05. Juli 2001, um 17.00 Uhr,
im Marmorsaal im Weißenburgpark in Stuttgart begrüßen zu dürfen.

Lassen Sie sich von unserem Programm überraschen und genießen Sie einen
abwechslungsreichen Abend mit geistigen und kulinarischen Genüssen.

Bitte geben Sie uns bis zum 15. Juni 2001 mit beiliegendem Telefax-Formular
oder telefonisch Bescheid.

TD

Thurm & Dinges
Planungsgesellschaft mbh
Friedrichstraße 10
70174 Stuttgart
Telefon (0711) 2 28 71-0
Telefax (0711) 2 28 71-49
Email info@thurm-dinges.com

Bitte vormerken: 05/07/2001

Thurm & Dinges Planungsgesellschaft mbH

Wir wollen mit Ihnen feiern, und zwar am 5. Juli 2001, ab 17 Uhr
im Marmorsaal, Weißenburgpark, Stuttgart. Was genau es zu feiern gibt
und ein detailliertes Programm inklusive Einladung werden wir Ihnen
im Mai zukommen lassen. Bis dahin.

D

Thurm & Dinges
Planungsgesellschaft mbH
Friedrichstraße 10
70174 Stuttgart
Telefon (0711) 2 28 71-0
Telefax (0711) 2 28 71-49
Email info@thurm-dinges.com
www.thurm-dinges.com

Title: 30th Anniversary Invitation Posters   Description: A1 posters inviting clients of an engineering company to their 30th anniversary dinner
Medium: Print   Date: 2001

Title: Hover Figure   Description: Sketchbook work for exhibition and personal use   Media: Pencil and Photoshop   Date: 2001

Title: Jedi   Description: Sketchbook work for exhibition and personal use   Media: Pencil and Photoshop   Date: 2002

remaining time **17** | **12** passengers seated

remaining time **32** | **9** passengers seated

Title: Airplane   Description: Game with air stewardess seating passengers   Medium: CD-ROM   Date: 2001

score 0 | 11 cups remaining

sound   game   story

Title: Tea Game   Description: Tea-time artillery game   Medium: CD-ROM   Date: 2001

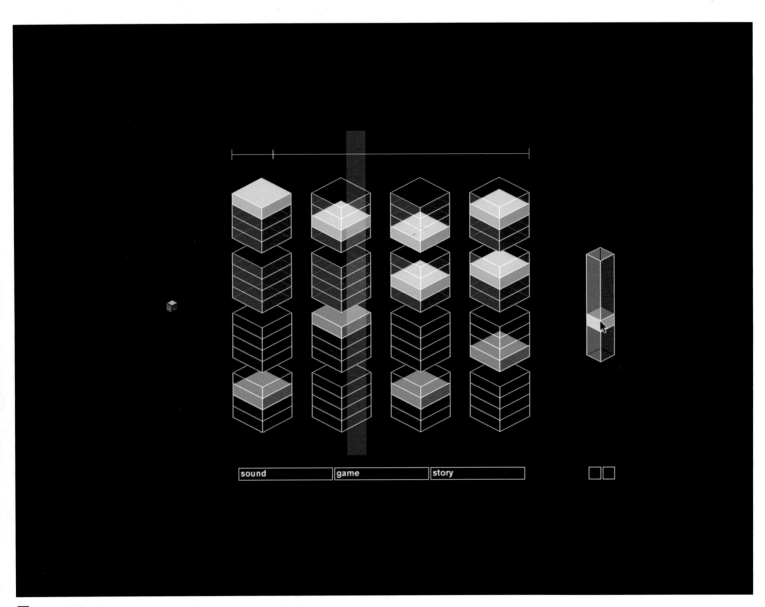

Title: Stacks   Description: Music-mixing toy   Medium: CD-ROM   Date: 2001

ROM AND SON

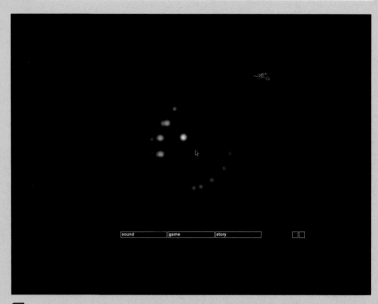

Title: Globe   Description: Interactive music toy   Medium: CD-ROM   Date: 2001

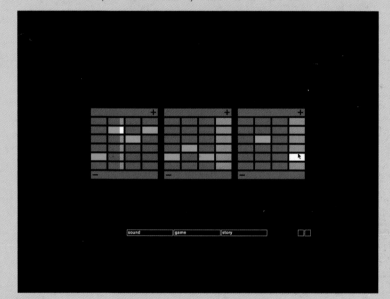

Title: Phase   Description: Interactive music toy   Medium: CD-ROM   Date: 2001

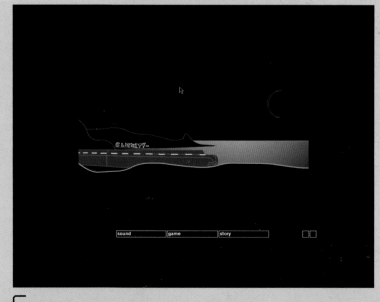

Title: Train   Description: Interactive story space on CD-ROM   Medium: CD-ROM   Date: 2001

Title: On Paper Exhibition, Crafts Council   Description: Die-cut stacks of paper for interactive gallery guides and section markers throughout the exhibition space   Medium: Print   Date: 2001   Photography: Andrew Penketh

1 Crease sheet into eight sections

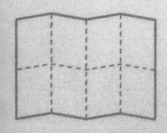

2 Fold into four with cut in centre

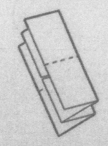

3 Open to form book

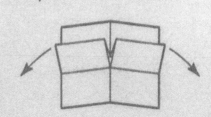

ossē

me

4 Finished book

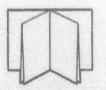

Title: On Paper Exhibition, Crafts Council Description: Die-cut stacks of paper for interactive gallery guides and section markers throughout the exhibition space Medium: Print Date: 2001 Photography: Andrew Penketh

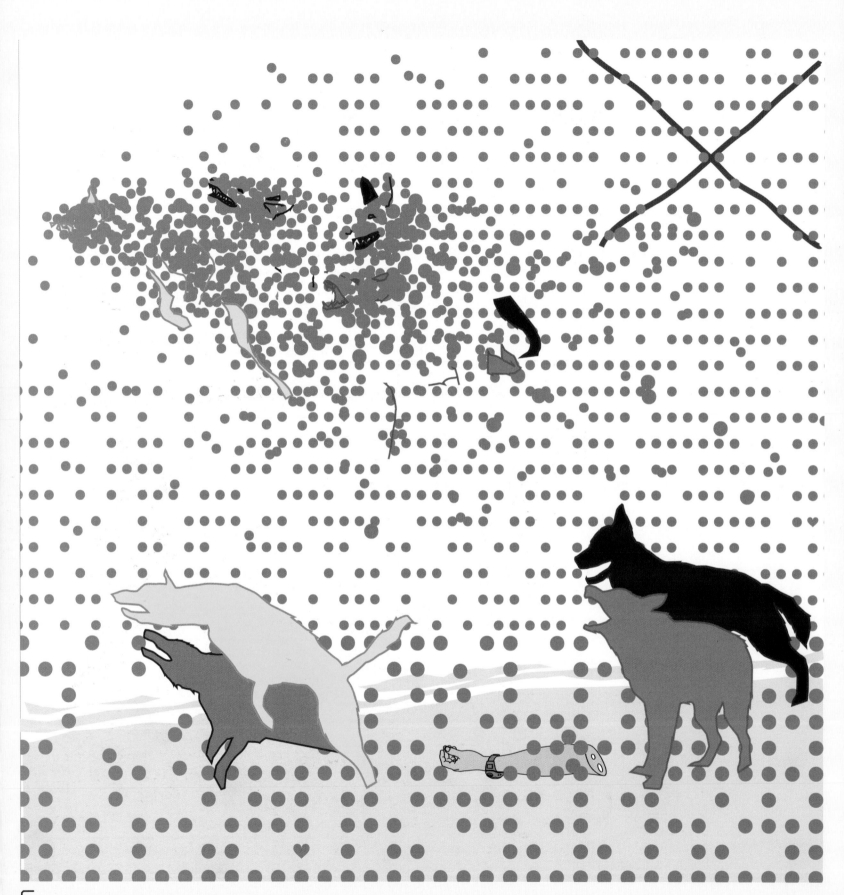

Title: Maybe Later (IV)   Description: Collaborative "visual Chinese whispers" project with 15 other designers – receiving and altering images, before passing them on   Medium: Print   Date: 2001

SHYNOLA

Title: Cowboys   Description: Illustration for Rank magazine   Medium: Print   Date: 2001

Title: Wonder   Description: Part of a series of personal responses to comics and superheroes   Media: Collage on paper   Date: 2000

Title: Sound Republic   Description: Promotional poster for Shynola's VJing night at a club in Tokyo, Japan   Medium: Print   Date: 2001

Title: Ever Fall in Love with a Machine?   Description: One of a series of images for a video pitch to the band Supergrass   Medium: Digital image   Date: 2001

Title: Private View   Description: A three-week-long billboard exhibition in Liverpool featuring the work of 15 Merseyside designers   Medium: Print   Date: 2001
Photographer: Mark McNulty   Coordinated and curated by Splinter and Rebecca Proctor   Billboard on this page designed by plast.cjacuzzi (Ged Doyle and Steve Hardstaff)

Title: View From The Window Description: Leaflet and programme covers for an exhibition celebrating life in the Everton tower blocks, commissioned by CDS Housing Authority Medium: Print Date: 2000 Photographer: Guy Woodland

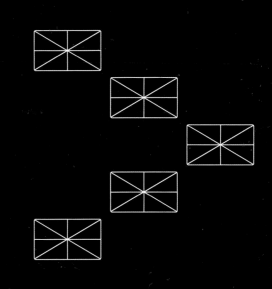

on air

Title: Hungry For Music   Description: Series of Flash animations for the website ‹mtvjapan.com›   Medium: Web   Date: 2001

music

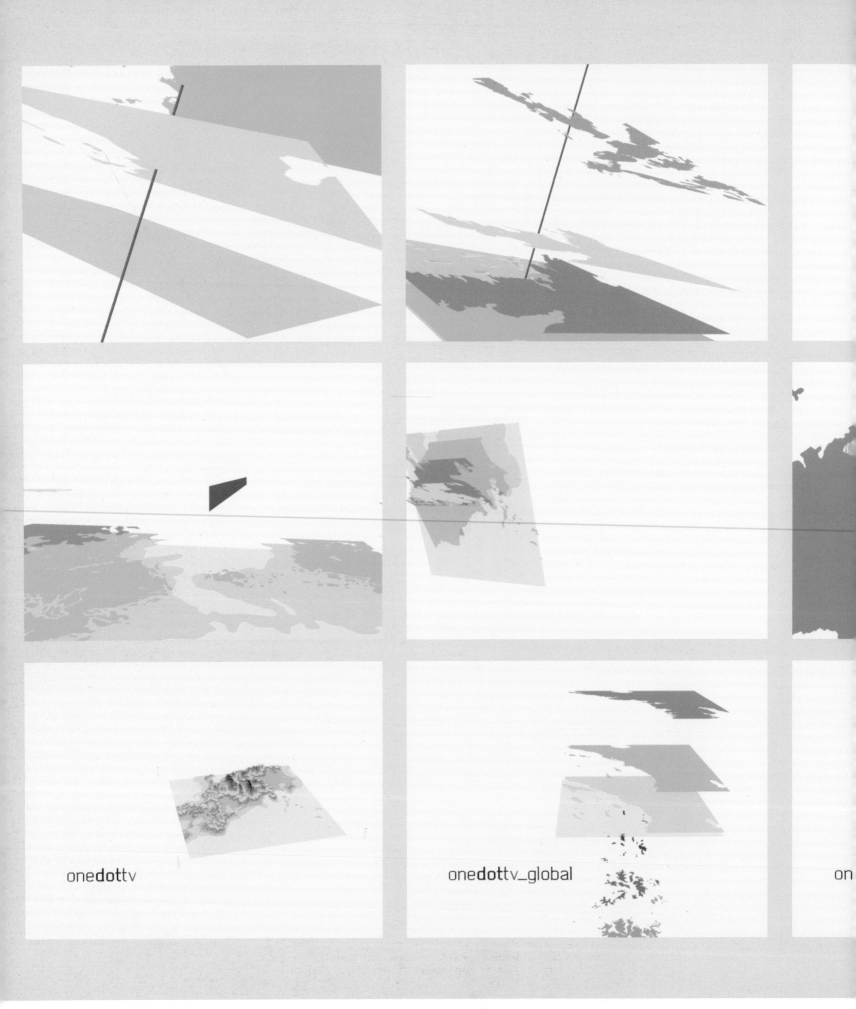

onedottv

onedottv_global

on

_global

pioneers of mov

Title: onedottv_global   Description: Title sequence to the Channel 4 TV series profiling international digital film-makers   Medium: Video   Date: 2001

Title: City Description: Computer graphics commercial for BT Cellnet WAP phones Medium: TV Date: 2000 Design: Marc Craste

Title: Fishing   Description: TV commercial made for Natwest   Media: TV and digital animation   Date: 2000   Design: Shynola

Title: Higher Learning   Description: Channel identity for BBC Learning   Medium: TV   Date: 2001   Design: Grant Orchard

Title: Oil   Description: Test commercial for Time magazine   Media: TV and digital animation   Date: 2000   Design: Philip Hunt

STUDIO AKA

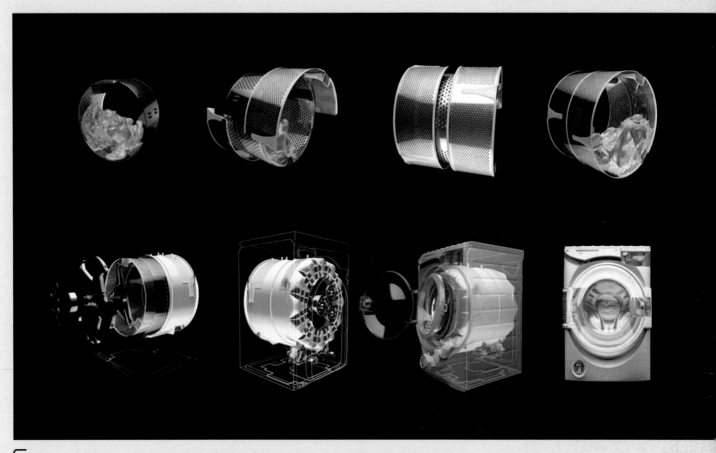

Title: Dyson   Description: 40-second commercial using computer graphics   Medium: TV   Date: 2001   Design: Philip Hunt

HANDBOOK

M_01

Title: Handbook for a Mobile Settlement   Description: Detachable and folding booklet designed for Grizedale, Cumbria   Medium: Print   Date: 1999
Photography: Harriet Sharkley and Donald Urquhart   Design: Paul Farrington   Artist: Jorn Ebner

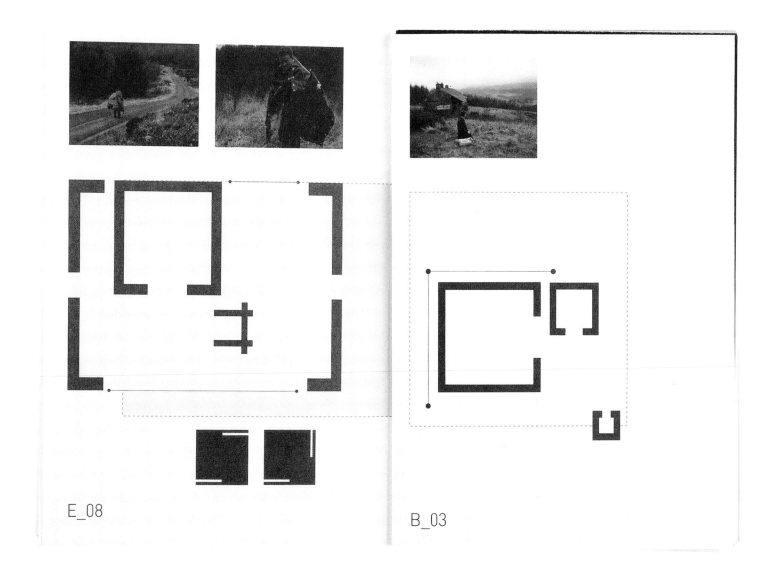

E_08

B_03

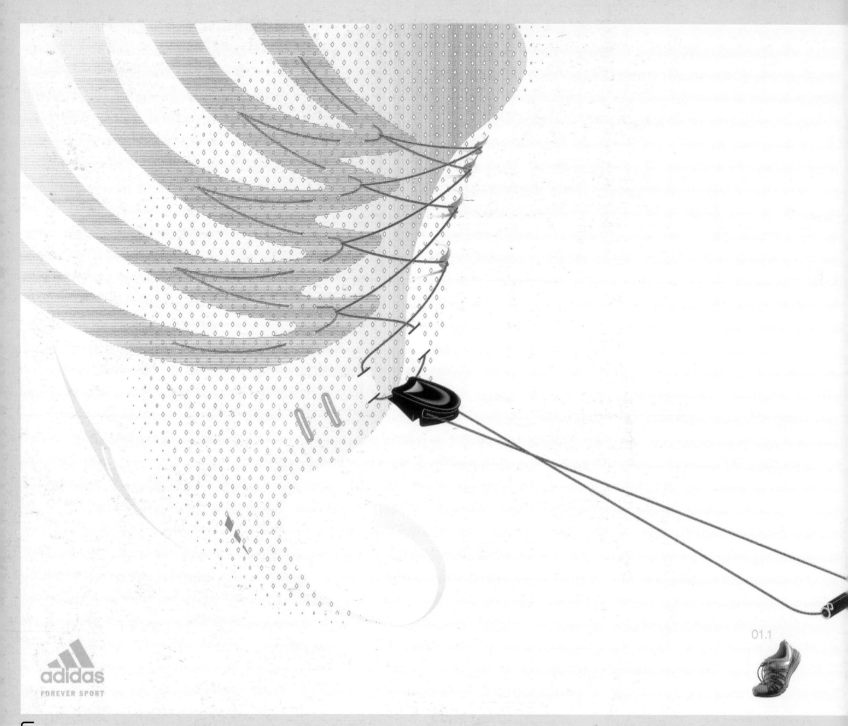

adidas
FOREVER SPORT

01.1

Title: Adidas Star Racer   Description: Part of a Bluesource design project combining art and science by reinterpreting the technology of Adidas trainers   Medium: Print   Date: 2001

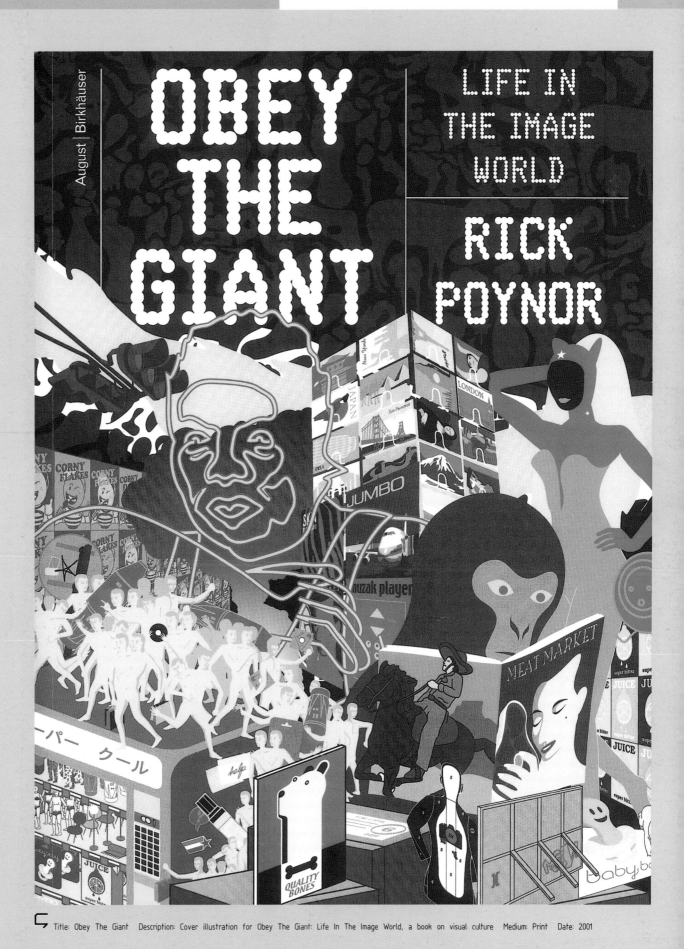

r Racer
n Lacing Technology
by Kam Tang

Title: Obey The Giant   Description: Cover illustration for Obey The Giant: Life In The Image World, a book on visual culture   Medium: Print   Date: 2001

Title: Vertigo Description: Tailoring fashion spread for Arena magazine 103
Date: 2001 Photography: Michael Williams Medium: Print

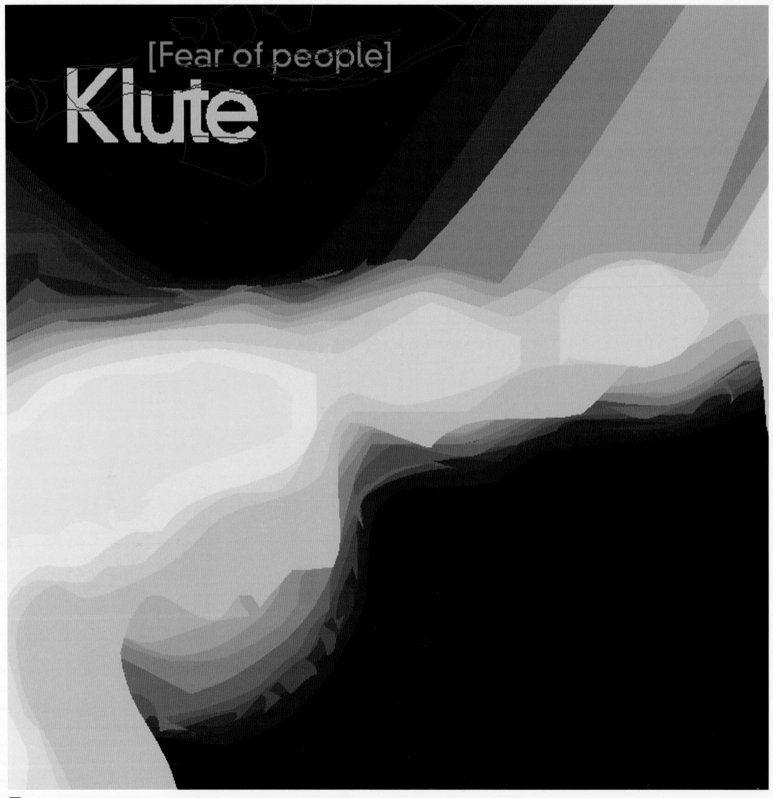

Title: Klute: Fear of People   Description: Front-cover design for Klute on Certificate 18 Records   Medium: Print   Date: 2001

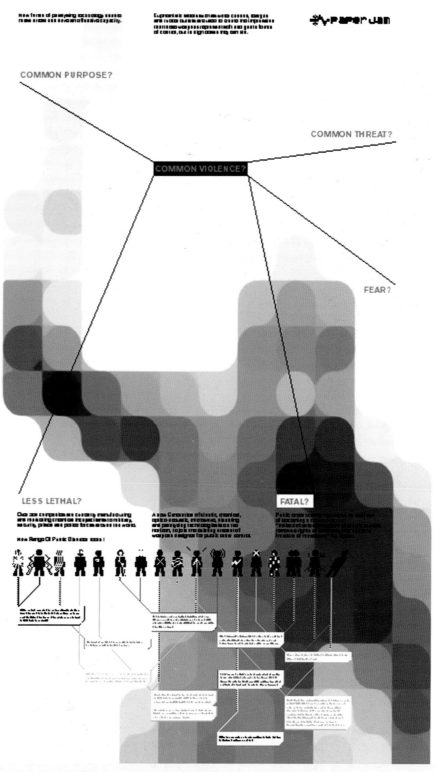

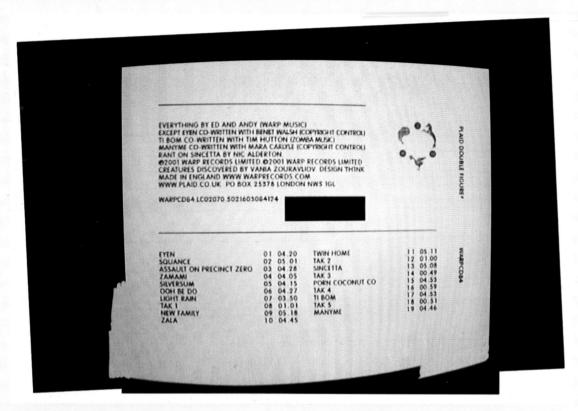

EVERYTHING BY ED AND ANDY (WARP MUSIC)
EXCEPT EYEN CO-WRITTEN WITH BENET WALSH (COPYRIGHT CONTROL)
TI BOM CO-WRITTEN WITH TIM HUTTON (ZOMBA MUSIC)
MANYME CO-WRITTEN WITH MARA CARLYLE (COPYRIGHT CONTROL)
RANT ON SINCETTA BY NIC ALDERTON.
©2001 WARP RECORDS LIMITED ℗2001 WARP RECORDS LIMITED
CREATURES DISCOVERED BY VANIA ZOURAVLIOV. DESIGN TH1NK
MADE IN ENGLAND WWW.WARPRECORDS.COM
WWW.PLAID.CO.UK PO BOX 25378 LONDON NW5 1GL

WARPCD84 LC02070 5021603084174

PLAID DOUBLE FIGURE*

WARPCD84

EYEN	01	04.20	TWIN HOME	11	05.11
SQUANCE	02	05.01	TAK 2	12	01.00
ASSAULT ON PRECINCT ZERO	03	04.28	SINCETTA	13	05.08
ZAMAMI	04	04.05	TAK 3	14	00.49
SILVERSUM	05	04.15	PORN COCONUT CO	15	04.53
OOH BE DO	06	04.27	TAK 4	16	00.59
LIGHT RAIN	07	03.50	TI BOM	17	04.53
TAK 1	08	01.01	TAK 5	18	00.51
NEW FAMILY	09	05.18	MANYME	19	04.46
ZALA	10	04.45			

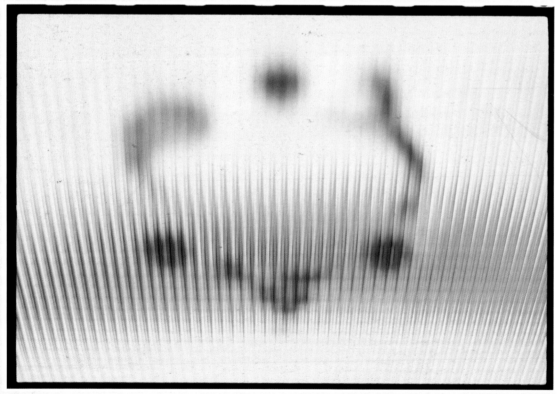

Title: Plaid: Double Figure   Description: Images taken from Plaid's album and CD booklet   Medium: Print   Date: 2001   Photography: Richard Burridge

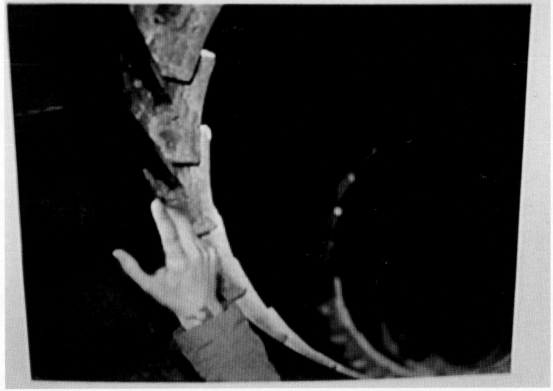

kettel.tadley management ep

www.planet-mu.com
ZIQ043.made in england
barcode 5036706000551

Title: Kettel, Tadley Management   Description: Sticker for the vinyl EP on Planet-Mu Records   Medium: Print   Date: 2001

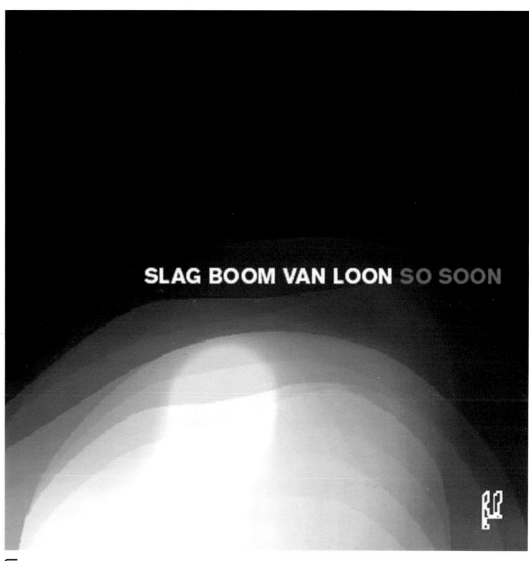

Title: Slag Boom Van Loon So Soon   Description: Cover design for CD release on Planet-Mu Records   Medium: Print   Date: 2001

GDR¹
CREATIVE
INTELLIG

Dilke House 1 Malet Street London WC1E 7JN
T +44 (0) 20 7580 5589 F +44 (0) 20 7580 5
E info@gdruk.com W www.gdruk.com
GDR Creative Intelligence Ltd Registered No. 2

CE³

⤷ Title: GDR Identity   Description: Company stationery designs   Medium: Print   Date: 2001

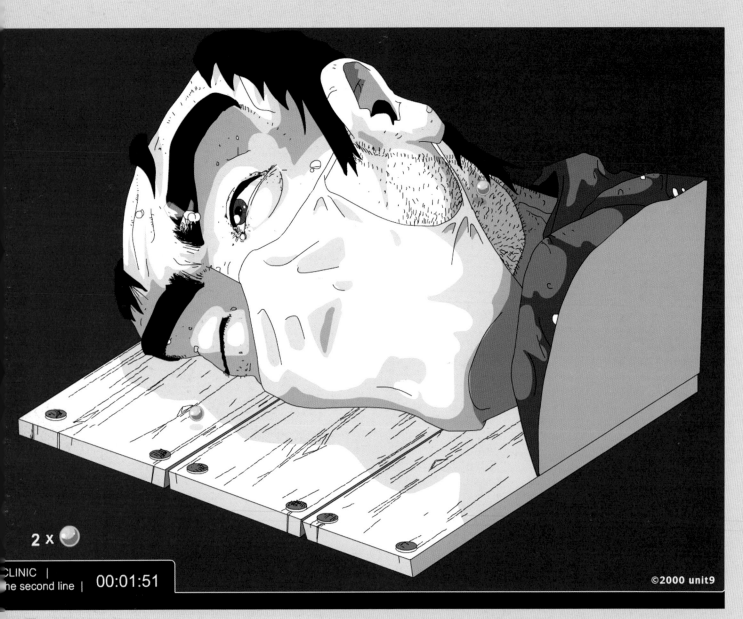

2 x

CLINIC |
the second line | 00:01:51

Title: Clinic: The Second Line   Description: Music video and web game   Media: Video and web   Date: 2000

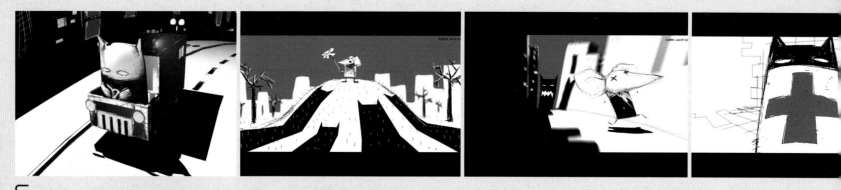

Title: Parasite   Description: 90-second animated short for the Sci-Fi Channel   Media: Mixed media   Date: 2001

Title: Full Moon Safari   Description: Flash5 animated short with 3D effect, as part of the unit9 series on ‹www.fullmoonsafari.com›   Media: Digital animation and web   Date: 2001

plus one

Title: Plus One Cover   Description: Record sleeve design for DJ Plus One   Medium: Print   Date: 2001

Title: Experimental   Description: In-house design piece for Unorthodox Styles   Medium: Print   Date: 2001

Title: Extensions   Description: Illustration for Mac User magazine   Medium: Print
Date: October 2001

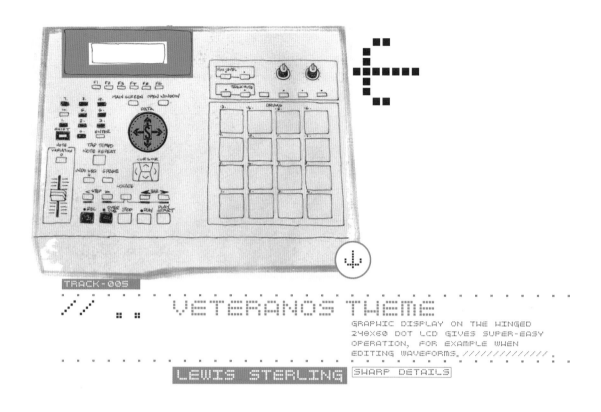

TRACK-005

// .. VETERANOS THEME

GRAPHIC DISPLAY ON THE HINGED
240X60 DOT LCD GIVES SUPER-EASY
OPERATION, FOR EXAMPLE WHEN
EDITING WAVEFORMS,/////////////. .

LEWIS STERLING   SHARP DETAILS

Title: Veteranos Theme   Description: T-shirt design for Lewis Sterling   Medium: Textile print   Date: 2001

>005

> appendix **A**: **The Art of Sampling**

Recording good samples is not always easy; creating a really super set of sounds requires patience, practice, and skill. Sure, you can get musically useful results within a few days after working with the **LSTR 005**, but as you learn your craft the quality of your samples will improve dramatically.

sampling involves two major processes:

*O1 Finding and abusing the best possible sample.

*O2 Manipulating the sample within the **LSTR 005** (truncating & looping).

> **LEWIS STERLING**

Title: The Art of Sampling   Description: T-shirt design for Lewis Sterling clothing label   Medium: Textile print
Date: 2001

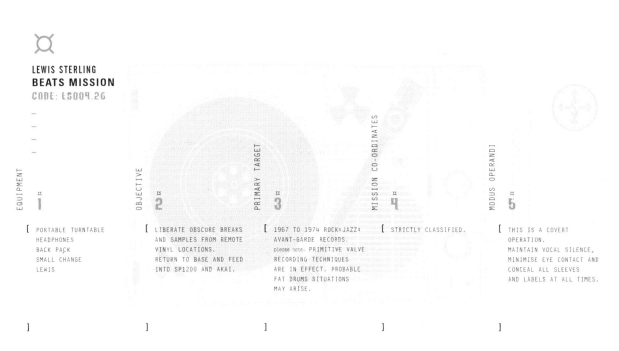

LEWIS STERLING
BEATS MISSION
CODE: ES004.26

EQUIPMENT
¤
1
[PORTABLE TURNTABLE
HEADPHONES
BACK PACK
SMALL CHANGE
LEWIS
]

OBJECTIVE
¤
2
[LIBERATE OBSCURE BREAKS
AND SAMPLES FROM REMOTE
VINYL LOCATIONS.
RETURN TO BASE AND FEED
INTO SP1200 AND AKAI.
]

PRIMARY TARGET
¤
3
[1967 TO 1974 ROCK+JAZZ+
AVANT-GARDE RECORDS.
please note: PRIMITIVE VALVE
RECORDING TECHNIQUES
ARE IN EFFECT. PROBABLE
FAT DRUMS SITUATIONS
MAY ARISE.
]

MISSION CO-ORDINATES
¤
4
[STRICTLY CLASSIFIED.
]

MODUS OPERANDI
¤
5
[THIS IS A COVERT
OPERATION.
MAINTAIN VOCAL SILENCE,
MINIMISE EYE CONTACT AND
CONCEAL ALL SLEEVES
AND LABELS AT ALL TIMES.
]

00.4

Title: Beats Mission   Description: T-shirt design for Lewis Sterling clothing label   Medium: Textile print   Date: 2001

Biographical information

A2-Graphics/SW/HK was set up in 1999 by Scott Williams and Henrik Kubel. Before meeting at the Royal College of Art, Williams studied at the University of Salford, while Kubel completed the five-year Graphic Design course at the Design School in Denmark. Since 2000, they have been based in London and have worked for arts and cultural organizations in the UK, while maintaining professional links with Denmark.

Airside was formed in 1998 in London by Alex Maclean, Nat Hunter and Fred Deakin, who all met in Edinburgh, where Hunter and Deakin had been at the University. Before completing their postgraduate degrees at the Royal College of Art, their collective studies and commercial work already included projects in human-computer interface psychology, English literature and interior design. They also have experience in architecture, interactive design, art, music and running clubs. These influences are significant in Airside's multimedia approach to design.

Peter Anderson @ Interfield Design Peter Anderson moved from Belfast to London to study for his BA and pursue postgraduate courses in Graphic Design, Fine Art Printmaking and Photomedia at Central Saint Martins College of Art and Design. In 1997, in partnership with Ray Leek, Anderson set up Interfield, and in 2001 he won the type design category at the Press Advertising Awards. Interfield now operates as a group forum for individual specialists, who represent all forms of media.

Automatic is a studio working in design and art direction for digital, print and spatial media. It is the creative vehicle of Martin Carty, who left Cheltenham to study for his BA at Central Saint Martins College of Art and Design, and of Ben Tibbs, who moved from Newcastle to train at the Glasgow School of Art. Automatic was set up in 1995, when the two designers met while studying for the Visual Communication MA at the Royal College of Art.

Nicholas Barba was born and educated in London, and went on to Central Saint Martins College of Art and Design to take the BA in Graphic Design. He completed his MA in Communication Art & Design at the Royal College of Art in 2000, and now works as a freelance designer, producing solo work and engaging in design collaborations.

Bark is the creation of Tim Hutchinson and Jason Edwards, both postgraduates of the Royal College of Art, who set up Bark on the completion of their studies in 1995. Since then, they have established a far-reaching design brief, which includes work for clients as diverse as Walt Disney and the ICA, London.

Beat 13 is a collective with four core members – Matt Watkins, Tim Watkins, Lucy McLauchlan and Al Murphy. In 1999, Matt Watkins, recognizing the creative potential in his friends, decided to establish a website for the group. The aim was to inspire them all and to try to get them some exposure. Together, Beat 13 cover design, illustration, web-based work, animation, music and more.

Big Corporate Disco was founded by Joseph Burrin, Justine Clayton and Tristan Dellaway, who had all been part of the design collective Guerrilla6, responsible for the original art direction on *Sleazenation* magazine. BCD was established in 1998, with Matt Clark completing this multi-disciplinary team, which specializes in 2D design, print and motion graphic media.

Bump brings together the talents of Mike Watson and Jon Morgan. Originally from Yorkshire and Essex, Watson trained in fine art at Brighton and Morgan studied graphics at Central Saint Martins College of Art and Design. They met at the Royal College of Art, where they collaborated on a College exhibition and publication. Through Bump, which was founded in 1995, they have continued their partnership.

David Burns was raised in Cumbria, then moved to London, where he trained in animation at the Museum of the Moving Image. At present, he works as a freelance animator, clean-up artist and illustrator on projects such as the *Clint Eastwood* and *Rock The House* music videos for Gorillaz, and the 2002 World Cup Manga sequence for the BBC.

CHK Design is the London-based design company established by Christian Küsters in 1996. Trained at the London School of Printing and Yale University, USA, Küsters now teaches at Camberwell College of Arts and is art director of *AD Architectural Design*. In 2002, he curated and designed the exhibition *Design Now Graphics* at the London Design Museum.

Neil Coxhill was brought up in Surrey, before going to study at Buckinghamshire Chilterns University College for a BA in Graphic Design and Advertising. Currently, he is signed with Harry Nash in London as a director and animator working on commercials and music videos, as well as continuing to work freelance in graphic design and animation.

Chris Cunningham was born in Reading and lives and works in London. His work has been shown internationally to great acclaim, and in 2002 he had solo shows in Berlin, Copenhagen, Dublin and London. His work was a part of the major exhibition *Apocalypse* at the Royal Academy in 2000, and he has created and directed music videos for Björk, Aphex Twin and Madonna.

D-Fuse emerged in 1995 with the media concept event *Chiaroscuro* and went on to create *The Wire* magazine website. D-Fuse are known for their projects in multimedia, from web design to motion graphics, and their work can be seen in clubs, exhibitions, print and on the Web.

Digit was set up in 1996 in Nottingham by Daljit Singh, who was joined later by Simon Sankarayya and Nick Cristea. The agency moved to London and now includes over 30 artists and designers. Merlin Nation, a graduate of Nottingham Trent University, joined in 1999. Digit works in digital media, including architectural installation, mobile communication and broadcast.

Draught Associates was established in 1997 by designers Michael Lenz (MA Royal College of Art), David Gibson (BA (Hons) Liverpool) and Paul Stafford (BA (Hons) Loughborough). Since then, Draught have developed their reputation in print, branding, environmental design, and screen-based and digital media.

Fat Ltd is a group of architect/designers led by founding partners Sam Jacob, Sean Griffiths and Charles Holland. The three met through their studies in Manchester, Westminster University, the Bartlett School of Architecture and Glasgow School of Art. Fat create work for commercial and gallery projects that explores the relationship between architecture, fine art and the city.

Richard Fenwick was born and educated in Newcastle, where he first studied graphic design at Newcastle College. His training then took him to Brunel University and, after graduating in 1997, he began working as a video graphic designer. In 1998, Fenwick co-founded the independent film company OS2 and, in 2000, set up his own creative studio called ref:pnt, which allows him to explore ideas and produce work, including the *artist in residency* programmes at Designafairs and short films for Warp and Rephlex.

Lizzie Finn is a Londoner born and bred. She studied for a BA in Graphic Design at Central Saint Martins College of Art and Design and now works on her own. Her work encompasses design and art direction (Moloko, Beta Band, Hysteric Glamour), fashion and editorial illustration (Japanese *Vogue, Dazed and Confused, Relax* magazines) and prints for fashion textiles (Silas, Frost French).

FL@33 is run by the multilingual design partners Agathe Jacquillat and Tomi Vollauschek as a studio for international and visual communication. Graduates of the Royal College of Art, they have worked out of Notting Hill, London, since 2001, producing work in publishing, exhibition and screen-based design. They have also created the annual architecture, art and design project *Trans-Form, Trans-It, Trans-Port.org.*

Fluid, established in 1995 in Birmingham, have recently extended their operations by opening an office in London. Founder James Glover co-directs with Neil Roddis; Lee Basford, Mark Harris, Ben Ridgeway, Chris May and Victoria Betts make up the rest of the Fluid team. Their work incorporates all media, with a strong presence within the entertainment industry.

Form is a London graphic design consultancy, directed by Paul West and Paula Benson. With their music industry background, they have collaborated with several major bands, their projects including the Everything But The Girl campaign, for which they won the Virgin Music Week Award for Best Art Direction. Form has seven members and works in experimental design for print, TV and the Web, as well as running the off-shoot clothing company UniForm, set up in 1997.

Foundation 33 was founded in 2000 by Daniel Eatock, a graphic designer, and Sam Solhaug, an architect, and now has a team of eight designers and writers. The two partners have both worked extensively in the USA and are now based in the UK, where Eatock holds the post of Senior Lecturer in Graphic Design at the University of Brighton. Working in all types of media, Foundation 33 produce projects for TV and screen, as well as in architecture, art and furniture design.

Josh Fuller (BA (Hons)) graduated from The Arts Institute, Bournemouth, in 2001. Since then, he has been working in music industry design in London, currently with The Homegrown Entourage in Brick Lane.

James Goggin works as a designer in the UK and New Zealand. He runs projects in London, Europe and Japan while co-designing for the clothing label Shan James, which he set up with his wife, Shan Connell. Goggin started Practise after graduating from the RCA in 1999 and continues to work predominantly in print and moving-image media.

Robert Green, from North London, graduated from Central Saint Martins College of Art and Design in 1996, before moving to the Royal College of Art, where he graduated in 1998. He lives and works in Hackney, London, where he specializes in graphic design, illustration and typography.

Johnny Hardstaff was raised in the West Midlands before moving to London to attend Central Saint Martins College of Art and Design. His work has been shown internationally and he has won an award at Cannes. He has produced visual work for Radiohead's *Amnesiac* album and is currently working on a digital arts feature film project.

Jon Hares studied at the University of Brighton, before attending the Royal College of Art. Since 2000, he has worked as a freelance graphic designer on many projects, including exhibitions and design ideas for promoting the arts and sciences. He is also Associate Senior Lecturer at the University of Portsmouth.

Tom Hingston Studio was founded in 1997 by Tom Hingston. The company now has four members, who specialize in music, fashion, publishing, TV titles and Web design. THS have been recognized for the art direction and design for Massive Attack's Œ *Mezzanine* and Robbie Williams' recent album campaigns. In 2002, the studio worked on a womenswear campaign for Christian Dior and designed a Rolling Stones album.

The Identikal Corporation was created by twin brothers Adam and Nick Hayes while at the University of Wolverhampton. On graduating in 1998, they took Identikal to their home town of London. Their projects, resolutely multimedia in approach, are international in scope and include the Guinness Storehouse in Dublin and Drop Club in Hong Kong.

Lee Jepson went from art school in Nottingham to Buckingham University, where he graduated in Graphic Design and Advertising in 2001. He now lives in East London and works in illustration and design.

K10k (and Kaliber 10000) were started by the award-winning Danish designers and Web developers Toke Nygaard and Michael Schmidt, who, together with Per Jørgensen, created Moodstats. In keeping with their international interests, they divide their time between London and San Francisco, while their work continues to be featured in books, periodicals and magazines from Hong Kong to Malmö.

Lab + Pavlova are the creative projects of Astrid Stavro Marone-Cinzano and Joana Ferreira Ramos-Pinto. After moving from Spain and Portugal to the UK, they continued their training in art and graphic design at Central Saint Martins College of Art and Design. The quarterly magazine *Lab* was first published in September 2000 as a medium to view the work of young artists in the areas of design, photography, music, fashion and architecture.

Less Rain was founded in 1997 by Vassilios Alexiou and Lars Erbele as a new-media agency based in both London and Berlin. Less Rain takes a multi-disciplinary approach and has over 30 members, bringing together designers, programmers, illustrators, sound engineers, photographers, architects and artists. Carsten Schneider and Thomas Myer make up the team.

Lucy McLauchlan trained at Liverpool Art School and has been living and working in London as part of the Web-based collective Beat 13 since 1999.

Rick Myers lives and works in Manchester. He took the four-year Art and Design course at Stockport College and has since produced work for the music industry, including sleeve designs for artists and record labels. As well as exploring ideas for the personal project *Footprints in the Snow*, with poster editions and sculptures, Myers designs for theatre, publishing, exhibitions and film.

Mysteriousal trained for three years at Falmouth Art College. Since graduating, he has continued painting and produces stickers, street installations and Flash animations for the internet. In recent years, Mysteriousal has been featured in several books and magazines, including *The Face, Lodown* and *CreativeBase*. In 2001, he became associated with the creative collective Unorthodox Styles.

Frank Philippin was born in Stuttgart, Germany, and, after graduating from the Royal College of Art in 1999, set up the South London-based design company Brighten the Corners. His time is divided between various visiting lectureships and creating innovative work for clients that include *The Guardian*, the ICA and the Crafts Council.

Steff Plaetz was born in Oldenburg, Germany, and brought up in Birmingham and Bristol, where he began skateboarding and creating art. At present, he is working on a number of canvases for the show *BOB* in New York, with other work being shown in Japan. Meanwhile, he continues to design for the clothing labels Satan Arbeit and Doarat.

Rom and Son was officially established in 1999 by Joe Stephenson, Andy Cameron and Andy Allenson, who had been working together for four years. The company creates interactive experiences delivered via the Web and CD-ROM and makes installation work that can be seen in retail spaces and museums.

Sans+Baum are Lucienne Roberts and Bob Wilkinson. Roberts studied at the Central School of Speech and Drama before realizing her true ambitions and training as a graphic designer at the Central School of Art and Design. After a brief period at The Women's Press, Roberts established the design studio Sans+Baum, her aim to work on projects outside the purely commercial. Wilkinson graduated from Central Saint Martins College of Art and Design in 1993 and started work at Neville Brody's Research Studios. After four years, he joined Roberts at Sans+Baum, where he is involved in a range of projects, from arts-related ones to charity-based work.

Shynola all met while studying Illustration and Media at the Kent Institute of Art and Design. Gideon Baws and Chris Harding began working in illustration and animation in London, while Richard Kenworthy and Jason Groves went on to the MA course at the Royal College of Art. With work featured in the UNKLE (MoWax) live show and their links with Studio AKA producing promos and advertising, Shynola was fully established in 2000.

Splinter was set up in Liverpool in 1996. After studying Video Art at Dundee and Staffordshire Universities, Chris Beer formed the company with Paul Musgrave. Now Splinter is run by Chris Beer and Nick Howe, with a staff predominantly trained in Liverpool at John Moores University. Splinter produce work in a range of disciplines, ranging from print, web and digital media to 3D design and visualization.

State is a multimedia graphics studio that was brought into being by Mark Hough, Philip O'Dwyer and Mark Breslin in 1997. Hough and O'Dwyer, who come from Cambridge and County Tipperary, Ireland, respectively, met and collaborated at Central Saint Martins College of Art and Design. Their first joint project was the art direction of *ORaise* magazine, and with State they continue to work on interdisciplinary collaborations, ranging from music, writing and code to design for screen, video, websites and print.

Studio AKA represents designers and directors producing a range of work in animation and commercials, broadcast and internet projects. Before becoming Creative Director of Studio AKA, Philip Hunt worked as an animation director in Stuttgart, San Francisco and London, while accumulating ten international art and design awards. Marc Craste directs commercials worldwide, and in 1999 and 2000 he won the British Television Advertising Craft Award for Best Animation. Grant Orchard is a director of commercials and he has won two D&AD Silver Pencils for his work designing interactive animation for the Web. In 2000, Kevin Meredith graduated from Buckingham Chilterns University, joined Studio AKA and won second place at the Lomo Olympics, Tokyo. Before becoming a member of Studio AKA, Jo Billingham worked as a freelance designer and artworker. Recently, she won a D&AD award for work on the interactive piece *Caffeine Society*. Shynola are recognized internationally for their work in short films, music videos and commercials.

Studio Tonne is the Brighton-based design company created by Paul Farrington in 1998. Having studied at John Moores University, Liverpool, and the Royal College of Art, Farrington now works in print and interactive media. He is currently writing and designing his first book on graphic design and the internet, and two albums, premiered in the exhibition *Sound Polaroids* at the ICA, are being released in 2002.

Kam Tang has worked as a freelance designer since graduating from the Royal College of Art in 1996. In 1998, he was awarded the Creative Review Futures Award for Illustration. He is currently working in advertising, editorial and music design.

Think1 is the brainchild of Richard Burridge, originally from Southend-on-Sea, who began the company in 1996. Now, with designers Annie Tidyman, Ben Curzon and Ruth Jobey, the Think1 approach is one of perpetual investigation and learning. Based in London, they specialize in graphic design for posters, music packaging and logotypes.

Unit was set up in February 2000 by Simon Parkes and now includes Neal Whittington. Parkes was born in Sheffield, but grew up mainly in the south of England, where he attended the Bournemouth College of Art and Design before studying at the London College of Printing. Whittington started life in York and went to university in Leeds, before joining Unit in 2001. Unit works for the most part with print graphics for a variety of companies, including Reebok, Casio and Virgin Atlantic.

Unit9 began life in Florence in 1997. The three co-founders and directors, Piero Frescobaldi, Yates Buckley and Tom Sacchi, grew up in Italy before their international travels for work and study took them, eventually, to London (via Boston). The original three-strong company now comprises 11 designers, with Mark Iremonger (via Dublin) and Ben Hibbon (born in Geneva) among the directors. With expertise as eclectic as their origins, Unit9 work as a digital production company in a variety of media, including updateable websites, digital marketing media and animation.

Unorthodox Styles is a creative agency made up of Ania Markham and the designers Chris Law and Chris Aylen, who both graduated from the London College of Printing. Mysteriousal joined in 2001, and the company produces a range of design work and personal projects, including <spinemagazine.com>, <spinetv.com> and <crookedtongues.com>.

BCD DT FN JF ID

BK DF LF FE TH

NB NC RF FD JH

AC DB PP F33 JH

A2 BP DT F@33 JG

LP

GRAPHIC BRITAIN
GB

SB

SA

U9

FM

LJ

SJ

RN

SE

UT

K10K

IL

CC

CHK

US

TE

FT

RG

LM

KK

SR

TK

SP

SJ

LR

ML

SA

KT

B13

Contact details

A2-Graphics/SW/HK
Unit G3, 35-40 Charlotte Road
London EC2A 3PD
T: + 44 (0) 20 7739 4249
E: info@a2-graphics.co.uk
www.a2-graphics.co.uk

Airside
24 Cross Street
London N1 2BG
T: + 44 (0) 20 7354 9912
E: nat@airside.co.uk
www.airside.co.uk

Automatic
Top Floor, 100 De Beauvoir Road
London N1 4EN
T: + 44 (0) 20 7923 4857
E: speak@automatic-design.com
www.automatic-design.com

Nicholas Barba
Studio 1, 63 West Smithfield
London EC1A 9DY
T: + 44 (0) 7966 283 771

Bark
Studio 2
East Block
Panther House
38 Mount Pleasant
London WC1X 0AP
T: + 44 (0) 20 7837 3116
E: bark@barkdesign.demon.co.uk
www.barkdesign.demon.co.uk

Beat 13
E: sifu@beat13.co.uk
www.beat13.co.uk

Big Corporate Disco
Unit 202
134–146 Curtain Road
London EC2A 3AR
T: +44 (0) 20 7613 3314
E: contact.bcd@virgin.net

Bump Associates Limited
Unit D
Flatiron Yard
Ayres Street
London SE1 1ES
T: + 44 (0) 20 7407 7482
E: bump@btconnect.com
www.bumptown.co.uk

David Burns
2nd Floor 14 Earlham Street
Covent Garden
London WC2H 9LN
T: + 44 (0) 20 7209 0275
T: + 44 (0) 7961 867 805
E: burnohbeard@yahoo.com

CHK Design
2nd Floor 21 Denmark Street
London WC2H 8NA
T: + 44 (0) 20 7836 2007
E: christian@chkdesign.demon.co.uk
www.acmefonts.net

Neil Coxhill
T: + 44 (0) 7710 490 320
E: random.task@virgin.net
E: markconway@battlecruiser.co.uk
www.neilcoxhill.co.uk

Chris Cunningham
c/o Anthony d'Offay Gallery
20 Dering Street
London W1
T: + 44 (0) 20 7499 4100
E: chiara@dircon.co.uk

D-Fuse
3rd Floor 36 Greville Street
London EC1N 8TB
T: + 44 (0) 20 7419 9445
T: + 44 (0) 20 7253 3462
E: design@dfuse.com
www.dfuse.com

Digit
54–55 Hoxton Square
London N1 6PB
T: + 44 (0) 20 7684 6769
E: info@digit1.com
www.digitlondon.com
www.digit1.com

Draught Associates Ltd.
133 Curtain Road
London EC2A 3BX
T: + 44 (0) 20 7739 3210
E: info@draught.co.uk
www.draught.co.uk

Fat Ltd
116-120 Golden Lane
London EC1Y 0TF
T· + 44 (0) 20 7251 6735
E: fat@fat.co.uk
www.fat.co.uk

Richard Fenwick
Studio 9, 87 Great Eastern Street
London EC2A 3HY
T: + 44 (0) 794 129 4170
E: richard.fenwick@virgin.net
www.richardfenwick.com

Lizzie Finn
20 Clink Street Studios
1 Clink Street
London SE1 9DG
T: +44 (0) 20 7407 8920
E: lizzie.finn@virgin.net

Fl@33
27 Hereford Road
London W2 4TQ
T: + 44 (0) 20 7313 9783
E: contact@flat33.com
www.flat33.com
www.trans-port.org

Fluid
1/222 The Custard Factory
Gibb Street
Birmingham B9 4AA
T: + 44 (0) 121 693 6913

London Studio 215 Canalot Studios
222 Kensal Road
London W10 5BN
T: + 44 (0) 20 8962 6216
E: drop@fluidesign.co.uk
www.fluidesign.co.uk

Form
47 Tabernacle Street
London EC2A 4AA
T: + 44 (0) 20 7014 1430
E: studio@form.uk.com
www.form.uk.com

Foundation 33
33 Temple Street
London E2 6QQ
T: + 44 (0) 20 7739 9903
E: info@foundation33.com
www.foundation33.com

Josh Fuller
15 Avondale Road
South Croydon CR2 6JE
T: + 44 (0) 7766 303 005
E: joshfuller@hotmail.com

James Goggin
Practise
T: + 44 (0) 7961 341 474
T/F: + 64 (0) 9 630 7278
E: james@practise.co.uk
www.practise.co.uk

Robert Green
Unit 53, 5th Floor
Regents Studios
8 Andrews Road
London E8 4QN
T: + 44 (0) 20 7241 0321
T: + 44 (0) 7989 569 973
E: i-bz@btclick.com
E: rob.green@cbgb.com

Johnny Hardstaff
RSA Films / Black Dog Films
42–44 Beak Street
London W1F 9RH
T: + 44 (0) 20 7437 7426
E: jhardstaff@rsafilms.co.uk

Jon Hares
T: + 44 (0) 7966 11 99 20
E: jonhares@btinternet.com

Tom Hingston Studio
76 Brewer Street
London W1F 9TX
T: + 44 (0) 20 7287 6044
E: info@hingston.net

Identikal Corporation
Studio 5, The Oasis Building
Empire Square
540 Holloway Road
London N7 6JN
T: + 44 (0) 20 7263 2129
E: info@identikal.com
www.identikal.com

Peter Anderson @ Interfield Design
2nd Floor, 21 Denmark Street
London WC2H 8NA
T: + 44 (0) 20 7836 5455
E: pete@interfield.freeserve.co.uk
www.interfield-design.com

Lee Jepson
T: + 44 (0) 7811 418 403
E: concreteyeba11s@hotmail.com

K10k
E: psst@k10k.net
www.k10k.net

Lab + Pavlova Ltd.
Lab Magazine
PO Box 31590
London W11 1ZA
T: + 44 (0) 20 7229 5105
E: info@labmagazine.co.uk
www.labmagazine.co.uk

Less Rain
Lincoln House
33-34 Hoxton Square
London N1 6NN
T: + 44 (0) 20 7729 7227
E: reception@lessrain.com
www.lessrain.com

Lucy McLauchlan
T: + 44 (0) 20 7229 0654
E: lucymc@yesmate.com
www.beat13.co.uk/lucy

Rick Myers Studio
23 New Mount Street
Manchester M4 4DE
T: + 44 (0) 161 953 4033
E: info@footprintsinthesnow.com
www.footprintsinthesnow.com

Mysteriousal
T: + 44 (0) 20 7734 6433
E: al@mysteriousal.com
www.mysteriousal.com

Frank Philippin
Brighten the Corners
30 White's Square
London SW4 7JL
T: + 44 (0) 20 7627 0868
E: contact@brightenthecorners.com
www.brightenthecorners.com

Steff Plaetz
T: + 44 (0) 781 699 0077
E: steff@scrawlcollective.co.uk
www.scrawlcollective.co.uk

Rom and Son
The Old Truman Brewery
91 Brick Lane
London E1 6QL
T: + 44 (0) 20 7770 6090
E: info@romandson.com
www.romandson.com

Sans+Baum
Unit 310, Clerkenwell Workshops
31 Clerkenwell Close
London EC1R 0AT
T: + 44 (0) 20 7490 8880
E: sans@dircon.co.uk

Shynola
E: info@shynola.co.uk
www.shynola.co.uk

Splinter
Unit 308 Liverpool Palace
6-10 Slater Street
Liverpool L1 4BS
T: + 44 (0) 151 709 9066
E: design@splinter.co.uk
www.splinter.co.uk

State
212C Curtain House
134-146 Curtain Road
London EC2A 3AR
T: + 44 (0) 20 7729 0171
E: staff@statedesign.com
www.statedesign.com

Studio AKA
30 Berwick Street
London W1F 8RH
T: + 44 (0) 20 7434 3581
E: info@studioaka.co.uk
www.studioaka.co.uk

Studio Tonne
71 Lincoln Street
Brighton BN2 9UG
T: + 44 (0) 1273 677 684
E: studio@tonne.org.uk
www.tonne.org.uk

Kam Tang
T: + 44 (0) 20 7737 1113
E: mail@kamtang.co.uk
www.kamtang.co.uk

Think1
167 Caledonian Road
London N1 0SL
T: + 44 (0) 20 7833 3933
E: thinkrich@easynet.co.uk
www.th1nk.info

Unit Design Consultancy Ltd
35-40 Charlotte Road
London EC2A 3PD
T: + 44 (0) 20 7739 8876
E: simon@unitdesign.co.uk
www.unitdesign.co.uk

unit9 Ltd
43–44 Hoxton Square
London N1 6PB
T: + 44 (0) 20 7613 3330
E: unit9@unit9.com
www.unit9.com

Unorthodox Styles
4 Ganton Street
London W1F 7QN
T: + 44 (0) 20 7734 6433
E: ania@unorthodoxstyles.com
www.unorthodoxstyles.com

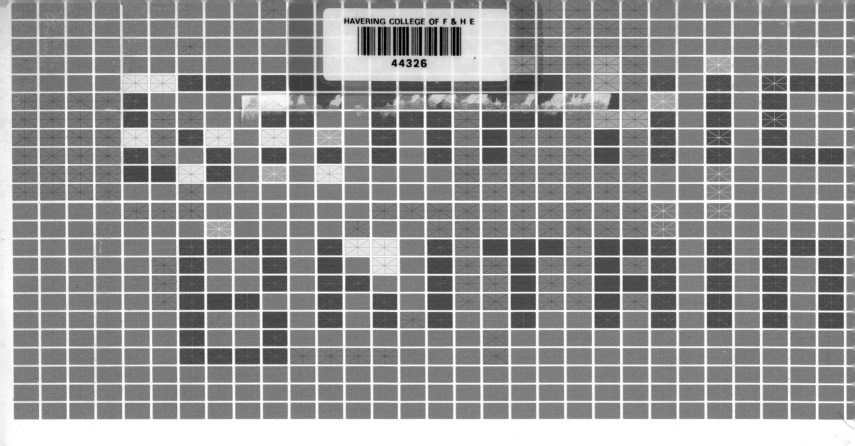